CROSSING AMERICA

Like No One Ever Has Before!

The Story of the First Amphibious Crossing of the United States

By Pedal-Paddle *Inventor*, *Road Warrior* and *River Pilot*, Jay Perdue

© Copyright 2004 – Jay Perdue

All rights reserved. This book is protected under the copyright laws of the United States of America. This book may not be copied or reprinted for commercial gain or profit.

Manufactured in the United States of America
(first edition 9/10/2004)

COPIES OF THIS BOOK MAY BE OBTAINED FROM

JAYVIC PUBLISHERS
4210 HESTER DRIVE
AMARILLO, TX 79124
USA

Toll Free 1-800-729-9402
Credit Cards Accepted

BOOK – PUBLISHED BY JAYVIC PUBLISHERS

Thanks!

At the risk of sounding like a broken record, I must first thank God. To me, that's Daddy of Jesus, without whose protection I would not be alive to write this book. He must have something left for me to do, like maybe turn 50 here in a couple of weeks!

Secondly, there's always my wife, Vicki. She puts up with so much and does so much. She says my guardian angels are going to "punch me out" when I get to Heaven. She's my opposite, my anchor, my lover and my friend. This trip caused us to be separated from each other both physically and emotionally more than anything ever has, which was my deepest and biggest regret. She came for the beginning, the middle, and the end, and made sure our companies stayed afloat in between, giving me the ability to make this trip in many different aspects.

Joab and Jesse, my two sons, are a great help to me. They inspired Pedal-Paddle to begin with and built the second one to prove it could be done, by my instructions, at ages 11 and 8 respectively. Special thanks to Joab who's recently married our little Pedal-Paddle model, Melissa. The boy's no dummy! And, thanks to Melissa for marrying him back!

Patrick Lee, our Pedal-Paddle manager, helped to procure the AEDC (Amarillo Economic Development Corporation) grant that eased our financial situation for this time in our lives and the life of the company. He also handled dozens of things both seen and unseen. Which leads to a big "Thank You!" to the AEDC, itself, for the $75,000 grant. I hope and pray that this seed will grow a huge crop for the city of Amarillo.

Thanks to Shawn for going along with me. He was not trained for the challenge at all, but took it on. I'll never forget that he was the one willing to go. When conditions required it, he stepped up and hit the ball out of the park when he had to.

Great encouragers along the way should be recognized as well. Without them, stepping in at just the right time with help, encouragement, or simply believing this whole thing would eventually work, I don't know if I would have made all the steps to Pedal-Paddle Across America. Joe Allen comes to mind here, as well as Ed and Shirley Armbruster, and my brother, James, and my brother-in-law and sister, Jim and Jacque. I have to admit I get a lot of spunk from my 92-year-old grandmother, Ruth Bell, and my remaining sister, Jennifer, the real athlete of the family.

My Mom and Dad have been married for 55 years, a tremendous feat in this day and age, an inspiration in many ways, and the reason for many talents and abilities, not to mention the fact that my incredible good looks come from them.

Thanks to my pastors, David and Connie Brown and Pat Brown, who challenge and inspire me as well. Many times I heard Connie's voice shout, "If you don't quit, you win!" I dedicate Chapter 18 to her, Chapter 17 to David, and anything fun about this book to Pat.

My office manager, Judy Andrew, a remarkable woman, proofs, revises and edits while Trisha types and Suzan retypes, and retypes, and retypes.... Thanks, ladies!

My friend, newspaper editor and now magazine editor, Debra Wells, revised, edited, and encouraged as well.

Finally, to all the folks at Pedal-Paddle, Perdue Acoustics and Jayvic Publishers who work so hard and consistently, led by Jayna, Russell, Joab, Judy, Jim K., Robert, Jim J., Vicki, Patrick, Juan and Tony, who allow me to do all the things God has called me to do. Thank you *all* so much and God bless you *all*!

Jay

Foreword

I want to thank all the news media that so graciously came out to write stories and do TV news interviews all along the way. From training in Florida, to the trek all the way across America, even through to my resting place on Huntington Bay, Long Island, the coverage was great and the enthusiasm for my crazy little invention was heart warming.

I'll never forget the hundreds of thumbs up, shouts of encouragement, and all the help and kindnesses people showed me along the way. This is truly an amazing land with amazingly good people. Thank you all very much.

Yes, I did see America in a way no one ever has before, on both water and land, and I wouldn't take anything for the experience. But, please remember this, almost never did a day go by that I didn't nearly get killed and some days several times. Only God knows, and I thank him for His protection.

The bright clothes and helmet, along with only riding in the daytime avoiding even dusk and dawn, were keys to my survival. But so was the fact that I'm infinitely familiar with Pedal-Paddle. I am trained as a pilot, have every road license available for the state of Texas, carry an advanced scuba divers certificate, and am bare boat sailing captain qualified, and was lifeguard certified and so on. Pedal-Paddle is intended for small lakes, rivers and ponds and in rural areas for getting there on roads. Certainly not for interstates, big waterways and big traffic areas on both water and road.

No one on the planet was more qualified than myself to make this trip, and even at that it would be considered a foolhearty and dangerous trip by most. Under no circumstances should anyone ever try to repeat what I've done. I am not saying this in fear of anyone doing this trek faster or better than I in any way, but out of sincere and genuine concern for your life. Everything in this book is as true and accurate a depiction as I could write, including this warning. Please, do not try to repeat what I have done; it is every bit as dangerous as I have depicted, and then some! Enjoy Pedal-Paddle in a safe way. Always wear a life jacket on the water and bright clothes and a bright colored helmet on land. You'll have all the thrills, fun and great times you can stand, and live to tell about them for years to come. Pedal-Paddle really is an awesome way to get to and play on the water.

God bless!
Jay Perdue

DAY 1 —Getting There-Getting Started

I hardly like to even waste my time with a chapter called "Getting There." In comparison to the actual crossing of the United States, getting there from our hometown of Amarillo, Texas, to our starting point of Seaside, Oregon, was somewhere between boring and frustrating. Boring in the fact that thousands of people have been cross-country in a motor home pulling a trailer of some sort, and frustrating in the fact that we had so many problems with the old girl, the motor home. I wanted this particular motor home for three reasons — sentimental value in that it was my parents' motor home when they first retired, expected dependability because it only had 63,000 miles on it and I knew it had been well taken care of, and thirdly because it was cheap! My second expectation (the supposed dependability) was the cause for all my frustration. The motor home was mechanically sound, but after my parents' many years in it, my brother living in it for a couple of years while deciding which lake in the Dallas area to build a house on, and the fact that it was purchased used to begin with, the motor home had multiple problems. However, in spite of these set backs, we made it, thanks to the handiness, resourcefulness, and know-how primarily of Patrick Lee, our Pedal-Paddle manager, and the tenacity of our Amarillo mechanics, Jody Rogers and James, his right-hand man. "Making it" required a 6-hour roadside service call six miles out of Amarillo, three fan belts, and several quarts of oil, but we made it!

Oregon is possibly the most beautiful state I had ever seen, and even before this trip I had been in all but four states. I marveled at its beauty and fertility, its varied crops and livestock, as we rolled along. I had planned to arrive on Friday so we could set up some bike dealership visits for Pedal-Paddle and kick off some media for the trip. We had done this very successfully in Florida while training, as well as in Amarillo as homeboy (me) got ready to go. My second intent was to head out Saturday morning so I could slide through a "quiet" Sunday morning in Portland. Since we arrived one day late, neither was accomplished and it almost cost me my life, but that's tomorrow's story.

We arrived in Seaside, Oregon, around 5:00 p.m. with just three hours of daylight left, and I was super antsy to get started. We found the Lewis and Clark Statue by the sea in the little village of Seaside and had to park our nearly 60-foot-long rig a couple of blocks away. We unloaded Pedal-Paddle Columbia out of the trailer and assembled it. I got dressed in my bright neon orange parka and helmet, and we headed quickly to the statue. Four to five foot waves were crashing on the beach, and the pre-season village was very quiet, especially for a weekend. We took a few still pictures and video around the statue in various poses and positions. There were nothing more than a few bewildered people looking at the strange "contraption" and the guy in the bright orange suit. They could have no idea what was beginning in front of them.

With no newspapers, no news cameras, and no fanfare at all, I climbed on Columbia. It was named for fallen Amarillo space shuttle Columbia pilot, Rick Husband. I pulled the engine start cord, pulled the throttle trigger and rolled off. As I rolled down the street with tourist shops on both sides, almost all were gazing at the strange contraption and the bright orange rider, and I just imagined they were all there to see me off. Not a one of them knew they accidentally saw the beginning of a planned two month trip that would set at least seven world records. All they saw that day was a strange sight. Behind the full-face orange helmet, I was nameless, unknown, mysterious, and even faceless!

The bicycle was fitted with the usual Pedal-Paddle pontoons, but a sailing bracket and, more importantly, a two-horsepower engine had been added for the trip. It whizzed me along, faster than the pedals could actually keep up with, at approximately 24 miles per hour on flat ground. It would only let me help on steep grades as it pulled down to a speed that my ability to spin the pedals could match. We buzzed through town quickly, without incident, heading south on Highway 101 for just 4 and a half miles along the coast and bay and finally the river that fed into it.

As we curved up and over to the east on Highway 26 towards Portland, it was like heaven. Gliding along, the speed was perfect for seeing every detail of my environment. Everything was so green, the trees so tall, huge and mossy, the stream so clear. The road had a nice but narrow shoulder, and cars and other vehicles passed by often, making me a little nervous at first, but my speed, factored into their speed as they passed by, made it all seem much less scary.

In the first 27 miles, Columbia and I had gone from sea level to 1,640 feet in elevation. The little engine was both a hit and a hero already, as I helped it only on the steepest inclines. Together, I felt we could conquer anything and we went really fast for a bicycle. The little engine was a four stroke, meaning it doesn't burn oil with the gas, usually quieter but always more efficient, not at all smoky, and "environmentally friendly," as they say. It was my new best friend.

One more mile past the coastal mountain range summit was home for the night. We found a beautiful roadside rest stop, picture perfect, with hiking and nature trails, a stream and very nice facilities. Columbia and I had gotten along so well on our first little jaunt; we had beaten the chase vehicles by 30 minutes! So we rested and answered the coming and going tourists' hundred-and-one questions.

Our beginning chase team consisted of my constant companion-to-be, 19 year old Shawn Nelson; my 19 year old son, Jesse; my wife, Vicki; and our before-mentioned manager, Patrick Lee. Upon their arrival, Pedal-Paddle was loaded into the trailer. We made a restaurant just down the hill and came back to the rest stop to sleep. It was our first night in the past three to actually sleep without moving or bouncing down the highway. It felt really good to lie still. My head hit the pillow with thoughts, visions, and pictures of great natural beauty. The first day was short but very sweet and I was out....

DAY 2 — Our First Full Day

What a kick-start! Today I find out if I can really make it. Could I go the distance? I made breakfast for the crew—hey, it's Mother's Day—and Vicki and I took a quiet hike. As we returned, Patrick was looking for us, all smiles. He grew up in Oregon and had found a patch of his boyhood treat. He called it "sour dock," cramming the leaves in his mouth and chewing. This convinced Vicki and I to at least give it a try. Strangely enough, it was kind of nice with a bit of a "sour apple" flavor.

We had the bike out and pontoons on in seconds, checked everything, and attached flashing amber lights to the back of each pontoon. I suited up in full weather gear as the elevation and longitude of Oregon felt cold to this Texas boy. I had several miles to head down the mountain. Today, I knew I would face faster downhill speeds and something even more frightening! The trip downhill was beautiful but fast, at times too fast. I braked often and coasted even more often, then I saw it: the tunnel! Not your well-designed interstate tunnel, just a long hole in the mountain with a sign above the black hole that said, "Turn Lights On." What lights? I looked back, checked my flashing amber lights, looked again to see if a car was immediately on my tail, and hit the black hole, praying that if a car or truck did come in behind me, they'd see the flashing lights and slow down. I checked my mirror frequently. It was a short tunnel, but at my speed it seemed like eternity. I saw lights enter the tunnel behind me, but I was almost to the other side. I cleared the opening and swerved to the shoulder immediately. Maybe a second later, the car shot past me! I wondered if I was ever in trouble or not. Was that routine for the car or did it ever even know I was there? The beauty of the mountains slowly washed the scary incident all away, and I had my old fear back soon…speed! I braked and got control as unbelievably beautiful mountains slowly gave way to unbelievably beautiful hills, farms, and gardens.

The roads merged more and more as I buzzed along, until I was on what seemed more like Interstate Highway 26, nothing at all like the little two-lane Highway 26 I had begun 60 miles earlier near Seaside. Ten miles from Portland, I was already getting into the city. Traffic was bustling and fast this afternoon. With most vehicles stepping the pace up to 70 miles per hour, the shoulder couldn't be wide enough for me and I hugged the right edge to get away from the roar as they passed. Truckers, normally courteous, were forced to hold their lane in traffic, and their turbulence rocked my little light craft violently at times. A lot of friendly, excited faces were plastered to the windows as they passed by the strange vehicle, and an occasional friendly honk and a wave or thumbs up told me they were impressed with my little contraption, but this all soon changed.

Highway 26 was now a full-fledged interstate and my worst nightmare was about to befall me on my first full day. Still just a baby to this world, it's not fair! Immediate and unexpected road construction squeezed all traffic to two lanes and *no shoulder*! Traffic slowed to 40 or 50 miles per hour but I topped out at 25 miles per hour. I sat on the edge for a while, considering the option of going back on the shoulder. Traffic jammed for a second and I jumped in! I held up my bright orange arm and bright orange glove and just jumped in as a car gave 50 feet to slow down for me. I jumped, they hit their brakes, and we were all one big, unhappy family. Just as I thought it couldn't get any worse, the construction went up a steep hill and I was down to 15 miles per hour pedaling speed, pedaling myself into a sweat and holding up traffic behind me. Trucks and cars and RV's blowing right by my left side, now back to 50-plus miles per hour, slowed only long enough to yell obscenities and blow their horns *at* me instead of *for* me. Needless to say, I was off at the first opportunity and out of their way, heart pounding like a deer being chased in the woods.

I regained my composure, thanked God *again* that I'm alive, and headed east! Now I was basically lost and off course, but I've always had a good sense of direction. Soon the "hit of the party" again, with comfortable traffic and city street speeds on a Sunday afternoon, I got lots of waves and heard, "Look at that, Daddy." My adventure went from "hell" to "well" again so quickly.

Floundering around on an eastwardly course, I stopped for directions to I-84 East after I felt sure I was comfortably east of the city. Although traffic was back to 70 miles per hour on the interstate, the wide shoulder was comfortable to me. I had heard rumors that Oregon did not allow bicycles on the I-84 shoulder. Stiff with tension, I passed a highway patrol waiting in the median to nab a speeder. He only waved back as I passed by and settled that issue, for now. Rooster Rock State Park was just 20 miles east of Portland, and I arrived 30 minutes ahead of my predicted time. With no chase vehicle in sight, I took off my heavy, bright orange suit. I hung the big overalls in a tree in the entrance so they could find me, lay the parka in the grass and stretched out to nap and give a tired, tense body a few minutes rest.

When the crew arrived, we went immediately to the boat ramp and launched Pedal-Paddle Columbia with its keels, rudder, and sail. The locals told us that usually the current and winds are both east to west, but today we fought the current with a light eastwardly wind. I knew the currents of the "great river of the west" would be too much for me, but this gave us the opportunity to at least try to get some time on the Columbia River. Currents in this portion of the river run up to six knots, so for a 4-knot maximum vessel like the 7'10" Pedal-Paddle, this was an impossible task. With the wind's help, I made about four miles in two hours and beached it for a carryout in what became four hauls up about a 100-foot embankment. This had not been the best of circumstances, but well worth our only chance to get on the westward-flowing Columbia River. After carrying and re-assembling Columbia with Patrick's help, I was headed back off east on I-84 to our campsite at Ainsworth State Park.

With the mighty Columbia River on my left and the cliffs and waterfalls of the Columbia River Gorge on my right, I felt as though I had passed from one heaven to another. The cliffs are so spectacular and some of the falls cascade down for what looks like hundreds of feet, truly breathtaking!

Our campsite was pristine and perfect. I don't know that I've ever seen a more perfectly kept and beautiful camp. It had one feature that I was desperate for, hot showers! Age had evidently taken its toll on the water heater in the RV. As a daily shower taker, I was plenty ripe enough to need a shower. The cold spring runoff water in the Columbia and the subsequent 10-mile ride at 25 miles per hour up I-84 had me chilled to the bone, and only hot water could thaw me out.

I bought $5 worth of firewood, and after the shower we built a campfire. The fire was blazing in no time, and Vicki and the boys showed up right about the time our campfire dinner was ready. For a guy who had ridden 90 miles on land and four against river current on a bicycle in a day, it was the perfect ending to a very long day. I slept soundly and peacefully, very pleased with the accomplishments of my first full day and that of my faithful and already proven versatile steed!

DAY 3 — A Long Day Up the Columbia

The Columbia River had proven itself a formidable foe in day two and, as predicted, not a wall I wanted to bang my head or my Pedal-Paddle against. We prepared Pedal-Paddle for the day and cooked out on a campfire Patrick had made for us. After a good old-fashioned camp breakfast of eggs, sausage and cheese all scrambled together, I kissed Vicki, hugged Jesse, my son, and Patrick goodbye. They had been indispensable in getting this "party" kicked off, but they were flying back to Amarillo after a day of bike shops and searching for a new RV water heater. All four of them, the motor home, and the trailer headed west, while Pedal-Paddle Columbia and I headed east. I was a little overwhelmed with being all alone for the first time on the highway without even so much as a chase vehicle, but it was a feeling I was going to have to learn to live with.

I was actually amazed to see it was just as beautiful a trek as the day before. I guess it almost seemed like a dream. Breathtaking beauty everywhere, and at 20 miles per hour and 180-degree visibility, I saw it all and took it all in. I wore a full-face motorcycle helmet with a visor, but I do not like glasses or goggles unless they're absolutely necessary. I wanted to see all of nature totally unobstructed, if possible.

My first "jumpstart of the heart" came only a few miles from camp with another tunnel. There I was on an interstate, and there was a tunnel that narrowed to only two lanes with *no shoulder*! Now remember, traffic was flowing at 70 miles an hour. I repeated what worked last time. I looked back to check my flashing strobes, waved my arm to indicate to over-taking traffic I needed a lane, and hit the tunnel in the right lane, 45 miles per hour *slower* than traffic! Now you have to understand this situation. If the car behind me saw me and slowed down in behind me, I would probably be okay. If the car behind changed lanes quickly and passed, the next car or truck in line would not know I was there and run in behind me at 70 miles per hour into a dark tunnel; an almost sure fatal accident. Traffic was light and I made it again, but I *hated* the feeling of entering these tunnels so vulnerably. All I could do was depend on traffic to see my bright colored helmet and clothes, change lanes, or slow down. Not a good feeling when my life was at stake.

As the day went by, the wind howled 30-plus miles per hour and the river actually had three to four foot whitecaps on it. The wind was at my back up the gorge, but the gorge widened into a steep valley more and more. Again, at construction of a bridge, I had to raise my arm and take possession of the only lane, depending on a fast-approaching car to slow down for me. He did, as did the diesel truck behind him. I got out of their way as fast as I could and waved my thanks to the driver. He waved back. I was glad for his understanding, and we all moved along down the Interstate. The speed was twenty miles per hour for me; they all accelerated past.

At 110 miles for the day, I pulled off of I-84 for fuel and a stretch. My back was really sore and spasming a bit. I'd been on the bike for almost five hours straight. My fill up was .75 gallons. That's 110 miles on three quarts of regular gas or just over 145 miles per gallon while traveling up river. Wow! In the first three days, if there was a hero emerging, it was this "little engine that could." It hardly ever let me help, it only asked for quarts of fuel and hasn't missed a beat in months of testing or since we started, going hours at a time.

So, with a fill up, stretch, and a bottle of juice, I was off again. I couldn't believe how quickly the vegetation changed as I headed east up the gorge and into the valleys. It happened so fast it was like I rode and slept for a time. The valleys suddenly had no trees at all, more desert-like bushes and rocks. The only thing that remained constant was the wind, and it was the cause of another close near-death experience.

I was getting used to the cars, trucks, and RV's blowing by me at 70 miles per hour, their turbulence sometimes catching my 18 lb. pontoons violently, but the wind was sneakier and almost got me. As a long curve to the right came around a cliff, I didn't notice that it had curved a full 90 degrees from the direction I'd been going. I came out from behind the cliff and a concrete guard wall at the same time to hit a 30 miles per hour side wind. It literally slid me sideways. My front tire skipped across the pavement and caught just as it started to cross the stripe in front of a diesel truck coming around from behind me on the same inside, *blind* curve. The truck swerved and just missed Columbia's left side. I literally shuddered and ached at the realization of what almost was! I just slowed to a crawl with my left foot hovering over the ground, ready to catch me as the gusts threw my little craft from side to side. The truck had just barely missed me; my fifth or sixth brush with death in the first three full days, and that's just the ones I knew about.

From there on, the wind was not my friend but a sneaky little villain out to take my life. I watched it like a hawk. I listened for it, watched its movement in the bushes and on the water to see what it might be planning for me next. I rode along cautiously, the wind along with the hours wearing me down and taking away the joy of the ride for a time. But the gale gave way, after a couple of hours, to become a breeze. I turned in its direction again, more northeast than east, and the wind at my back became my friend again, but a friend I would always have one eye on.

On Highway 730 Northeast, I passed by pigs, horses, cows and river valleys, so Americana it'd make you cry. Simple folks don't know how good they have it sometimes…or maybe they do. As 730 continued its trek along the mighty Columbia River, it never got less spectacular, it only changed its appearance. It became a canyon again with only the river, a train track, and the highway running through it. A two-lane highway with nice shoulders and a few cars and trucks driving along the way, I got the feeling more people should come this way and see these sights. Sometimes the "unadvertised" highways are the best.

After crossing into the state of Washington, Highway 12 headed back east again towards Walla Walla. Here, there was a little climb out of the river canyon that required a good bit of my help. The engine needed help and I needed exercise. What a beautiful valley, and a stream ran through it. Crops so green they redefined the word. A hidden surprise was on the hills to my right as a row of three-bladed wind generators that seemed five miles long and 100 feet tall beat the wind out of some of its power for us humans to use.

It was dusk now, and I checked my flashing rear strobes for safety, praying for a quick close to my day as rain sprinkled me. My prayers were answered as I rolled past more and more structures indicating I was coming into Walla Walla. I was an hour ahead of my chase vehicle, so I settled into a local restaurant, ordered food and waited, making a few calls to let everyone know that I was okay. Mathematically, I knew it was possible that if everything was perfect I could make 200 miles in a day on land. On this, my third day, I just rode Pedal-Paddle Columbia 220 miles! Shawn arrived soon and we bedded down in the restaurant's parking lot, with the owner's permission. Wow, what a day! *"Good night, Columbia. You done good!"*

DAY 4 — A Rainy Ride

This day I awoke to the sound of rain on the motor home's roof over my head. After yesterday's 220 miles "in the saddle," I was content to lie there for a few minutes and just enjoy the sound of the rain. I rolled out of bed, discovering new pains with every movement, and found pen and paper. Passing the time, I spent two hours writing the first three days of this book. Taking a call from one of the local radio stations, my main message was "Tell all the folks in the area, especially the truckers, thanks. They've been very courteous on the road," and they really had been. Shawn and I prepared Columbia quickly, too quickly, and had to return a half-mile for air in the rear tire. The rain was slow but cold as I headed back down the two-lane towards Lewiston, Idaho...100 miles. I really planned to go farther, but in the cold rain, I would see how it went. The farms in the region were nothing less than immaculate. My hands were the only thing that minded the cold rain...well, and my face. Ducking my head so the rain would miss my eyes was only a partial fix as that inhibited my vision, and the rain still hit my cheeks and ran down my chin and neck. Still, the gentle rain was softened somewhat by the beauty of the many shades of deep green around me.

The black pavement gave way to black gravel sloping only a few feet to crops of every variety. The pictures in my mind of the homes and farms amazed me as I thought back at what I saw today.

I went through one small town and would like to pay a little tribute here. A girl, I don't know what age, was killed on a bicycle on this very highway the day before I went through. It was hard for me to forget this, and I was truly saddened by the news. I pray I can find a way to remind kids to wear bright clothing and a brightly colored helmet when bike riding as I have. I know it saved my life every day.

Then came the roller coaster ride. I helped Columbia climb like the chain ride to the top of a roller coaster, and then over the top and down we came. The rain had stopped by now, and with clear vision I gave Columbia her reins time and time again. Don't tell Vicki, but I'm pretty sure that I approached 50 miles per hour several times. It just felt stable and ready to fly. I'm pretty sure of my speed because I looked in my rear view mirror periodically to see if I was holding someone up. I'd see a car a quarter of a mile back that would take quite a while to catch me. I hit my brakes when it looked good for them to pass, hugged the shoulder, let off and flew again. One run, according to the sign, was five miles long.

A few miles out of Lewiston, the road dead-ended into the Indian River and headed sharply right up the canyon. A beautiful rocky mountain view with houses, nice houses, perched on hills overlooking the intersection. I rolled through Clarkston to a lot of stares and pointed fingers. With no shoulder, I led the pack down Main Street but my speed was near the legal limit of 25, so no one seemed upset with my leading. Through a light, the bridge led me into downtown Lewiston and the state of Idaho. I called Shawn to find out that he was 30 minutes behind me. I found a restaurant I thought he might like and ordered pizza. We ate, recapped the day and planned our evening.

I was not at all happy with the rest of my day. It ended around midnight. I used the world record-setting Columbia to chase down parts for the motor home, again, and worked for hours putting on another alternator belt, again. A new hot water heater was installed after yet another run for more parts to finish the job. Ah, the life of a record-setting superstar, riding all day, working on the chase vehicle all night...*I'm beat...good night.*

DAY 5 – Disappointing Day, Great People

I left Lewiston, Idaho—you know, right across the river from Clarkston, Washington—this morning. Get it? *Lewis*ton, *Clark*ston. Man, the folks all across this region were Lewis and Clark fanatics! And well they should be. These two men opened up the whole North West to the settlers, and everything in between.

Anyway, I made it a whopping 10 miles when the bike started to wobble. I used my two little cans of flat fixer for bikes and, boy, were they worthless. But both cans got me down the road to a "sportsman's river access" where I found several empty vehicles with boat trailers and one really nice gentleman with a hand pump. Bicycle tires, surprisingly, take about twice the air pressure as car tires, but the hand pump got the job done and me sweating. This was good for another five miles or so. I pulled into a group of four or five houses, knocked on the doors and hit the jackpot. Not only a little cigarette lighter powered pump, but also a car-sized can of flat fixer! This kind gentleman insisted it all be a gift and wouldn't take my ten bucks. I rolled on with my extra half can and bought more five miles up the road at a lone gas station. Now I was on a roll with one and a half cans of pure gold and an open road. All went well for 15 more miles, and then three miles out of Orofino, a sudden gunshot sent the bike nearly out of control. I steered like a drunken man staggers to the side of the road, surveyed the damage and hiked back a quarter mile to an out-of-town shop I had just passed. There, I informed the office of my whereabouts, as Shawn could not be found. Since I was brain dead, the nice lady also offered the suggestion I call the local tire service and ask if they would come and pick me up. "What are the chances?" I thought as I planned my begging and pleading. I made the trip sound as big as possible, and the local folks answered the call in absolute kindness. In minutes I was loading the bike up and was whisked off to a store to buy an inner tube and then to their tire shop for free tools and assistance. Four hours later and another trip to the store for a tire as well, and they presented me with a bill for $11!! I pleaded with them to charge me more and tried to slip my helper $5, but it was a "no go." The friendly folks of Orofino, Idaho, wouldn't hear of it!

So if you're ever in the area, give your business to Les Schwab Tires and go by and see all the nice stuff at Tyler's Metal Arts & More.

I still hadn't seen my chase vehicle in spite of attempts at letting folks know the only way I could how to find me. So I took off down the road and made another 20 miles. One thing the guys at the shop convinced me of was to not go past Kamiah, Idaho, without knowing where the RV was. *Good idea.* It was 150 miles ahead of me. It passed me while I was spending four hours fixing the blown tire and tube, so there I sat in Kamiah, penning this, but not until after a great Mexican food meal for this ol' Texan and another nice lady at the Clearwater 12 Motel who listened to my sad tale and insisted on giving me the trucker's special on the room. Oh yeah, the 50 or 60 miles was a beautiful drive up the Clearwater River, but who could notice that much with all the commotion?

Hey, isn't it great when you have a disappointing day to meet some really great people? Besides, I got to soak my aching back for an hour in a hot tub and stopped and bought the 500-count bottle of Ibuprofen. Ain't life grand? Tomorrow I'll do 150 miles the locals call "straight up the mountain." I was excited about the scenery and maybe the "little engine that could" would let me help for a while. *Good night, folks!*

DAY 6 – Miserable!

I knew this could be a challenging day, but I had no idea. I wanted to be sure to give myself enough time so I started out at 7:00 a.m. I was cold, *really* cold. My eyes teared continually and my fingers ached almost from the beginning. The river crashed over boulders with such violence I knew this was where the pros come to white water raft. Not just a little here and there, but an almost continual motion of violent force.

Running along the river was an amazing sight, but I had problems concentrating on anything but the cold. I had on thick neoprene divers' gloves with my bright orange insulated rubber gloves over that, and still my hands were so stiff from the cold I wondered if I would be able to move my fingers to the brakes and squeeze if I had to.

I began to exercise my fingers inside the gloves as best I could, just for such an emergency. The "little engine that could" chugged along nicely and I helped on the steeper inclines that presented themselves from time to time. At 30 miles I stopped for gas, knowing my next opportunity would be 60 miles further up. When I say up, I mean up. The total climb was 102 miles *up* from where I started, and I can't recall a single flat or downhill piece of road in the entire distance.

Something good started to happen on this stretch of road, however. Maybe it was the cold, the bicycle with the bulky pontoons, all alone in the mountains. Maybe I had gone enough distance to be "real." It started last night at the restaurant, then again here at this gas stop with river rafters and retirees alike, but everyone wanted my story and to take pictures of Pedal-Paddle Columbia and me. I handed out brochures on the company and the little amphibious craft to much accolades and positive feedback, many times for them to be handed back with a pen for me to sign for "when I became famous."

Anyway, it was flattering and encouraging, and helped greatly to keep me going and my spirits from crashing in the relentless cold. I hoped for sunshine and for a warm up. It never came. As the morning turned to noon, I climbed higher and higher, and it seemed to just stay the same. Not much sunshine but no freezing rain either. Sixty more miles up the mountain went by slowly, but another fill-up at a lodge/ranger station got me off the bike and into a warm gift shop for five glorious minutes.

Some days and some times pop up just to see if you've got what it takes to really get the job done. After more pictures and telling my story in brief, it was time to hit what was reported to me the last 12 miles up. "Six miles just like you've been going, and six miles of hell."

"Hell" sounded good to me after being chilled to the bone all day, so I took off determined to crest the machine and win the coveted prize of "mountain pass accomplished." It was just as the gift shop/gas attendant had reported. When it started "up," it was steep. For the first time, the little engine gasped and wheezed even as I helped all I could. We choked the hill down together until it finally gave up. A few more cranks on the pedals, and I knew I'd just have to get off and push it the last three miles. My legs were burning; hell had taken its toll.

I sat huffing and puffing for a minute. To my amazement, I was dripping wet under my bright orange suit, my hands no longer frozen but still cold. A divinely-inspired idea hit my little oxygen-deprived brain that saved me. I strained to retrieve my pocket pliers out of my suit and took off the air breather from the engine. I redressed with fully unzipped everything and pulled the starter cord. The little engine came to life and we were a team once again! It was three more miles of "hell" but we made it, snow all around by now and flakes beginning to fall. I rested Columbia on a snow bank and fell on my back with no one to videotape or record my trophy in any way. I got to my feet, zipped up my suit and continued on my trip, reverting immediately back to the same icy-fingered, bone-chilling world I had known all day. The instant downhill speed put me right back in the deep freeze, but I wouldn't go back to where I had been for anything; my legs wouldn't allow it.

Many more miles later, I came to a busy intersection, stumbled off the bike, got my bearings and headed the last eight miles into Missoula, Montana, where I spotted the RV and trailer in a Wal-Mart parking lot. Shawn and I rejoined, corrected the mistakes that created the confusion, and had a great "all you could eat" dinner. As the blue grass band played its merry melodies with much skill and precision, I was swept away from my day of misery. It was over...thank God, it was over!

DAY 7 – Another Pass!?

Oh yeah! This time, the Continental Divide! But let me just tell you now it was nothing compared to the pass in Idaho. No snow, I took the breather off for the summit, still burning legs and dripping wet but a piece of cake compared to the day before. The weather was great and although it was the same 90-mile climb, the "little engine that could" did most of the work. Sure, it was long and I helped a lot, but the day before had toughened me a bunch. The only annoyance was the state of Montana introducing me to a several mile section of what they called "grooved shoulder." This is basically a rumble strip that goes all the way across the stinkin' shoulder of the road! Thankfully there was only about 10 miles of it. I ran down the edge of the "good stuff" until my mirror reflected several vehicles coming back up at me, and then I moved over. Single vehicles were forced to move their wrist to the other lane. You can see I got an attitude after a while. If you're reading this, learn a lesson. It's so easy, especially on four lanes, to move over and give folks on the shoulder room to work. Just move your little arms a little flinch and do it. Believe me, no matter who it is or what they're doing, it's much appreciated.

Would you allow me to digress to yesterday? I have an interesting note to add. When I got off the road for fuel yesterday at the ranger's station, I went into the restroom. Looking into the mirror I noticed all under my eyes was pure white. Upon closer inspection, it was a white grainy powder-like substance. You may be used to this or experienced it many times, but in my almost 50 years, I had not. My eyes had teared so much for so long in the cold air at 20 miles per hour that my face under my eyes was white with *tear salt*!

Well, I had tear salt again today and was excited to be able to show Shawn I hadn't gone crazy the evening before with my "tear salt" story.

Another part of yesterday's story was left for today. It needs a little explanation, so bear with me.

You see a bicycle's gears are made to only drive forward. The way they slip to give you a second's rest on flat ground is the same way they slip down hill. Unlike a car or truck that can use its gears and engine compression to slow you down, the bicycle only has brakes. Pedal-Paddle Columbia is a heavy, four and one-half foot wide, eight-foot long, bulky contraption on a bicycle.

After a rest and a little video on top of the Continental Divide, I started down the pass to Helena, the capital of Montana. Yesterday I had allowed Columbia to race down the backside of the pass to reduce my time exposure to the cold and had gotten dangerously fast, but in stable air. This day was to start out similarly.

As I picked up speed, I knew I would get to a point where wind resistance and downhill gravity would equalize itself. Today that speed was well over 50 miles per hour! I was racing down the mountain like a downhill slalom ski racer. As I leaned and swooped through the curves, the valley spread out wider and wider. An occasional mild turbulence shook Columbia and sent me scrambling to lean and keep control.

I braked only on occasion to keep from burning out the light bicycle brakes and keep the speed manageable around curves. The two large pontoons sliced through the wind efficiently, but caught side winds like a sail. I came around an outside curve into open air on the side of the mountain. The wind pushed me into the oncoming traffic lane! I leaned hard right to come out of it as the wrong side of the highway flashed by off my left shoulder. The big contraption overcorrected and I headed for the guardrail, made to keep only people *inside* vehicles safe.

The rail would catch Pedal-Paddle and send me flying over and plunging down the steep side. I leaned hard left again. Columbia responded again with the right pontoon almost scraping the guardrail, just inches away.

The convulsing from side to side had slowed the machine considerably so I rolled on with stability, checking my invention and myself for damage. It seemed we had pulled it off unscathed and unbent, another possible death experience narrowly escaped!

The pass leveled to a more gradual down slope, and I sped down occasionally windy slopes to Helena where our first TV crew was anxiously awaiting our arrival. The TV station in the Montana capital was very nice and modern for a city of this size and the folks very efficient, congenial and professional.

We made our goodbyes around 5:00 p.m., and I moved on through town and up I-15 in search of a camping spot. I longed for a campfire and campfire-cooked dinner. It did not come without a price. The one and a half hour trip became a two and a half hour grind into the wind and up two very long hills, the first of which was almost equivalent to the Continental Divide with the addition of the wind.

The reward was two-fold. As I-15 turned to true north and fell off into a beautiful, rugged canyon, I was amazed all over again. The ancient creek had cut through purple layers of rock like a knife, leaving a narrow but deep canyon with just enough room in it for the road and the creek that had gone before it.

As it opened up, I saw the chase rig to my right at an exit and soon had the lowdown on which direction Shawn and I might find the camping spot of our dreams.

Fifteen minutes on down the old highway, we crossed both an old bridge and the most beautiful piece of slow-moving river you ever saw. It was in a wide valley with sunset just an hour away. Perfection. Shawn helped and toted as I whipped up steak, taters, and corn.

We sat by our little campfire to a most beautiful view of mountains and sunset. Better than any human being deserves. We couldn't leave until every gathered stick was gone. "No writing tonight," I thought. I'll do it in the morning. Nine hundred forty miles and two mountain passes done. It's all down hill from here. *Good night!*

DAY 8 – 1,000 Miles Done!

"Did you hear that, Shawn? Shawn, wake up! Did you hear that?"

Just outside our motor home, couldn't have been more than a few feet, a male elk bellowed again and again. I know there's a word for it, but I've never heard the sound before. Shawn described it as "somebody roasting a dog alive." That seemed pretty close, but it's not a painful sound, particularly.

Anyway, it was more potent than any rooster, and we were up and about. Shawn got up cooking and I got up writing. It wasn't long before we were both finished and eating his well-cooked ham and eggs. My appetite had become as ravenous as when I was a teenage boy, and I scarfed down the breakfast quickly.

We couldn't leave camp without explaining our strange contraption and trip and passing out a brochure or two, but soon I was suited up and flying down the recreational road at my steady 20 miles per hour.

I stayed on the recreational road for 30 miles or so, fearing the tricky morning mountain gusts. The interstate cut straight to Great Falls while the recreational road followed the river out of the mountains. I envied the interstate's speed and directness, but this recreational road was what it was all about.

As I buzzed along, pedaling often to help in the wind, I thought back over the last few days. Everybody was getting there faster than me, but I doubted it would even be possible for them to have seen what I had in the going: the ducks on the water's edge, a dozen or so deer hiding just off the highway in a little clearing, the geese with the baby goslings all in a row behind, the fields of baby calves and moms and their interplay that only 20 miles per hour could have given time for. Now as I whirred along, it was fishermen in various floating devices or just wading along, all looking up to wave at the strange sight of Columbia and its bright orange rider.

At the last of my "recreational road" travel, I enjoyed the full cycle of a helicopter in obvious fire fighting training as it was piloted down to a river pool, picked up water with a huge bucket dangling on a cable, raised it out, flew off, dumped it and came back for more.

I circled back up onto the interstate for the final 30 miles to Great Falls and witnessed, with mixed emotions, as the Rocky Mountains lay down their fight. They had been a formidable foe, but Pedal-Paddle had finally bent them down and conquered. They had many good punches and two walloping knockout blows, but they had been too predictable to be effective. We knew what they were up to and stopped every blow they threw at us, and we had won!

They were laying down the fight slowly but surely, and as we reached Great Falls, they were nothing but hills. I love the Rocky Mountains and hated to see them go with all their beauty and all they had shown me.

The river was ahead, but it was time for a break, so Shawn and I grabbed a hamburger and sat with a really nice local couple that wanted to know more about what we were up to.

We were disappointed to find that our previously excited local news media people were scattered for the weekend. Being a smaller town, the local television stations keep only a skeleton crew on for weekend news, so we slipped through town unnoticed to the masses and headed on to Fort Benton and the "Upper Missouri National Scenic and Wildlife River." Man, I liked the sound of that!

The wind changed its tactics against us. It couldn't trick us in the first few rounds; it now attempted to wear us down. I pushed 25 miles into the wind. It was like going up a pass, only longer in duration and not as hard as the summit. We endured and were winning until a different wind brought us to our knees. It was the sound of air coming out of Pedal-Paddle Columbia's back tire. I pushed it a quarter mile or so to a flat spot on the shoulder and off the road in traffic, caught an undependable roam signal on the cell phone and found Shawn back in Great Falls with the motor home as well. "It won't start," he said.

A local rancher/horse trader picked Columbia and me up in his pickup. The ride scared me to the point of white knuckles. I had gone over 1,000 miles at 20 miles per hour and 70 miles per hour took me by complete surprise. I found myself clutching the door handle with my right hand and putting my left hand on the dash to brace myself, all the while looking over to see just how fast we were going. We were back in Great Falls in no time. Three hours later, we were fixed on both accounts and heading back down the highway to where we came to a quick halt.

We pulled off the highway into a field at mile marker 25, where I spent two hours earlier that day, and crashed into bed. The road was calling for me to complete the last 12 miles to the river and then 40 miles on the river tomorrow. The state publication recommends 20 miles a day, so 40 seems about right for world travelers like Pedal-Paddle and myself. Until next time—see you after my first day on the river!

Oh yeah! I was so excited I almost forgot. One thousand miles to Great Falls! One thousand miles in four hours short of a week! That's incredible, but I owe it all to "The Little Engine That Could!"

DAY 9 – Our First Day On the River

My first day on the river started out with an hour on land, finishing from the previous day's flat tire spot into Ft. Benton. The wind was howling out of the north, and anytime the road curved enough for it to get a sideways push on me, it sent me scrambling for stability. It was all that the little engine and I could do to push into the wind, and more than a couple of times I felt Columbia slip sideways on the pavement.

As we arrived at the river, I spied the statue of Lewis and Clark and Sakakawea, the Indian woman who led them over the pass to the west. To my surprise, the statue of her had a little papoose on her back, a fact I was not aware of in the research I had done of the Louis and Clark expedition. We enjoyed an opportunity for video at the statue and then moved immediately to the water.

Several curiosity seekers gathered as we prepared Pedal-Paddle Columbia for the water. We passed out brochures of our creation, and Columbia and I launched quickly. The river was fast and an island was immediately downstream, so I fired up "the little engine that could" and it came to life on water as dependably as it had on land.

Soon we were zipping past the shoreline, clumsy at first, but I had Columbia under control and in the middle of the river, nose downstream. I had so hoped for a pleasant experience but it was cold, very cold, and very windy.

I had made a bad choice in donning a wetsuit, hood, gloves and booties. Made for being *in* water, they seemed very poor at keeping me either dry or warm. The wind kept messing with us and trying to throw us off course, but with persistence I held true to what seemed the best waters. Many times I would see rocks below. Mostly it was a rocky bottom of the smooth, round, fist-sized variety. Although often 6" deep, the 3" draft of Columbia cleared easily. I had no fear of this as the tire protected the paddles very well.

I increased the throttle a bit and found I had more control, but this bothered me because the pace the engine was putting out to maintain control was not a pace I could keep up with on my own. If it ever quit, I would not be able to control the craft well at all under such severe conditions.

I thought the wind would be much better down in the river canyon, but it seemed to sneak around every corner and find new ways to twist and swirl and wreak havoc. On one turn, I found myself increasing throttle until the little engine was shooting a rooster tail of water back 20 feet or so.

At times the river slowed down and at times raced along, but it seemed to be in control, taking me with it, in spite of Pedal-Paddle and I being only three inches into its world and three feet into the wind's world above.

The wildlife was abundant, as expected. I would need a book to describe and name all the species of ducks, geese, swans, pelicans and other birds along the way. The wind and water-worn cliffs were beautiful, with great variety of texture and color. An occasional fish would dart from beneath me back into the deep. Visibility was only a couple of feet, so I never knew beyond the frequent view of round stones flashing by below me what depth the pools might be. It was reported to me by one of my last-minute trainers back at the launch site to be "several feet deep most of the time."

As I stated earlier, I wish I could stay focused on the beauty and describe it more aptly, but quite honestly, I was miserable. I began to shiver and shake with nothing less than hours ahead of me with no way out. The sun was cruel, as it stayed just behind the edge of the clouds above all day. It teased me, breaking into blue a time or two, but never did come out fully or long enough to thaw me out. The wind grew worse and worse until the river lost its battle with the wind, and the wind took control. I found myself in a mile-long pool of river that seemed to not be moving at all. The winds whipped down the long canyon creating two-foot plus whitecaps beating directly at my 7' 10" long craft.

I felt a little sick and hopeless as I shivered, shook and looked at the insurmountable odds and canyon walls. Could I ask more of the little engine?

Already throwing a stream of water back 20 feet and 10 feet into the air, I squeezed the trigger a little more. I had created a little plastic air breather protector for the engine but was afraid that to ask more of it would create such a wild spray that it would literally choke itself out.

I had no choice. It had no choice, and the "little engine that could" lived up to its name once again. I felt like it was saving my life as it shot spray back 30 feet and propelled us slowly but surely against the wind and down the canyon. It was crawling speed, but every time the little engine momentarily even sputtered I held my breath. The river wouldn't let us go back, the wind wouldn't let us go forward, but we pushed down the long pool anyway. Little by little, foot by foot, we struggled against the wind. Then we turned the corner and I kept close to the high bank. Protected from the wind, I picked up speed and soon I recognized the "take out" we had planned.

The designated checkpoint, called "Wood Bowan," was 21 miles down the river from where I started at Fort Benton. I piloted Columbia to the gravel embankment, shut down the little engine, grabbed some shore with my feet and the small craft with my hands all in one motion, and hauled it up on the shore. Shawn was nowhere in sight, but I was grateful to be off the river. I poured one gallon of water out of the left pontoon and two gallons out of the right, not bad for a four-hour trip that took six hours and spent much of the time in two-foot waves. And don't forget, these pontoons had bounced down the highway for 1050 miles, which had to have had a chance at loosening them up as well.

I secured all the pieces of Columbia up the embankment, walked to the launch site entrance and waited for any sign of human life. There were only two other vehicles in the primitive, dirt parking lot, waiting on brave rafters to come down. Everyone else was either too afraid or too smart; I think the latter was right.

I waved down two gentlemen in a roaming pickup, and found out that Shawn had pulled up to the dirt road leading in just one mile down river and stopped. He was concerned about the deep ruts in the narrow passage leading down to the launch and retrieve site. They let him know where I was, and it wasn't long before I heard the dirt bike roaring towards me. I traded with him and rode the motorcycle back up to the motor home and trailer. I loaded the motorcycle back into the trailer, fired up the RV, and began a slow descent down to the river to a secluded little campsite. We gathered wood for a campfire and began cooking supper, a nice, warm and beautiful ending to a bitterly cold day.

Tomorrow I'll try my familiar orange parka and bib overalls, with a lifejacket to keep them from pulling me under. The occasional sprinkling of Pedal-Paddle's rear paddles doesn't even compare with the light rains I've been through. Going back to what worked on land is a better choice, I think, for staying warm and dry. I didn't come here to scuba dive the river, and I wasn't planning to swim or fall in, either. *We'll see how it goes with the "land clothing" on the water tomorrow. I want to spend more time looking and enjoying and less time shivering and chattering! See you tomorrow.*

DAY 10 – Breathtakingly Beautiful!

When I suited up at 7:15 a.m., all I wanted was a day on the river where I could be halfway comfortable. From my experience the day before, I was determined to stay warm even if it killed me…literally. I put on regular baggy jeans and a tee shirt and socks, and then pulled on the heavy bib overalls and mega parka I had bought for the Rocky Mountains in spring. I pulled my "Nanook of the North" boots on over the dry socks and as I did, this thought went through my head, "If I fell in, all this will weigh 100 pounds or more." I didn't care; I selected an "extra large" life jacket that would slip over the whole garb. I put on the leather-insulated gloves from my winter street attire and pulled the orange insulated rubber gloves over that. I could hardly move, but I was warm.

Shawn had Columbia ready, so in the early light we pushed it to the launch area and made it ready. I zipped up tight under my chin, pulled over the hood of my parka with only a little circle of my face showing and pushed out into the fast-paced current. I flipped the "on" switch, pulled the cord and the "little engine that could" purred to life. I had placed zip ties around the trigger to set a half throttle speed on the engine. Any more energy would be messy and wasteful. At this setting, the paddles threw back their 20-foot "rooster tail" and we were off.

Within the first mile we passed under the Loma Bridge. Immediately after, two deer were waiting to thrill my early morning launch and make my day. Puzzled by the sight, just as humans, they looked almost too long, and then danced their white tail dance down the beach, then stopped to look again. Friend or foe, man or all machine? They pondered for a moment or two more. Then my eyes, peering out of the little hole of the parka hood, must have given me away and they bolted off through the trees.

Birds of every shape and size became a constant part of the trip, and a curious otter swam along with me for at least a half mile. Cautious at first, he would dive and come up closer and closer until he was finally 40 to 50 feet away on my left side.

I was toasty and warm, and convinced I had river-conquering attire. The wind was calm today and the ride could not be more perfect. I had planned with Shawn that if I could make Coal Banks Landing by 12:30 and if the weather and wind stayed nice, we would do an "Indy 500" style pit stop and I would go for a river record.

At 12:30, one mile from Coal Banks Landing, I ran out of gas. Based on the previous day, this should not have happened, especially in this weather, but it did. I pedaled in my bulky suit and stopped and yelled for Shawn every 100 yards or so. No response, so I took the fast side of a little wooded island. On the other side of the island, with no fuel, no engine and a swift current, was Coal Banks Landing, the motor home and Shawn standing on the bank. I peddled furiously across the current, instantly breaking out in a profuse sweat. I made the shore just 50 yards or so down from the motor home, and it was Shawn's turn to sweat.

Like a trooper in battle, he ran back and forth with supplies, gas, tripod, and camera. I stuffed, poured and tied, and in no more than 10 minutes, I pushed back into the current again.

I knew my decision was risky, but I considered the odds as best as I could. I would take a pitch-black night over the howling winds like the day before, anytime.

This section of the river was "advertised" as the most scenic and beautiful yet, and it instantly lived up to its name. Breaks in the canyon walls revealed gorgeous views of the distant mountains, the cliffs were full of color and the wild birds seemed to be in even greater abundance.

I hadn't gone far when I experienced the thrill of the morning all over again, with a twist. Two bighorn sheep scrambled along the cliffs by the water's edge; quite a sight!

Just like the deer, they would scramble to and fro for a few seconds, look back to see if they really needed to hide, and then go back to jumping and sliding and tossing about on the cliffside. It looked as though they might take a tumble any second but they never did, and finally they darted up a steep canyon to hide.

I had seen only one lone kayaker since we had started the river the day before and so was surprised to come upon a string of canoes, one after another after another, for *miles*.

The landscape changed as well. More and more rugged, more and more carved, more and more weathered; until it took little imagination to see castles, sculptures, stone walls and all types of things in the rock and sitting on the rock. It was as though some ancient people spent their lives for generations stacking up boulders and carving rock into all types of fantastic shapes, just for our enjoyment and fascination.

With the whir of the motor and knowing I would have no time for chitchat, I nodded politely as I passed by the canoes, posing often for pictures of my strange craft and myself. I stopped once or twice for groups of several canoes to explain my journey and just figured they'd pass it on around the campfire that night to the others.

It went on this way for hours: still, beautiful, whirring along with a conservative 20-foot rooster tail off the back of my contraption. I planned another "Indy 500" pit stop carefully: emptied both pontoons, filled all three tanks, made ready the flashlights, and put important things for night river travel on top of the bags.

I pulled Columbia up on the bank and went about all my tasks with vim, vigor, and vitality, knowing a minute now would be a minute longer in the dark. I had just enough fuel left for two tanks so I planned my strategy as I tied the fuel can back to the pontoon support and pushed back into the water. I had just achieved another ten-minute pit stop and was off chasing the fastest current in the river again.

The weather could not have cooperated any better, but the river, I had noticed all day, was painstakingly slow. One by one, the canoes all left the river to make camp until I had it all to myself again. I loved the slow ride down as the sun got lower and lower in the west and began to cast magical shadows on the already mysterious surroundings.

But magic slowly turned to nightmare as it grew darker and darker. There was no moon at all, and the stars provided almost no light to the dark canyon. I strapped on my "headlight," a neat little gizmo that with an elastic band around my forehead would shine light in any direction my head was turned. I cut the engine but continued to drift in the night as I poured the last of my gasoline into the back two tanks and clipped the third tank's hoses shut with paper clips. I moved with great caution, knowing that a dropped cap or a slip on the pontoon as I maneuvered around in my 5' x 5' world could end in disaster.

After securing the gas can again, I pulled on the cord, praying that "the little engine that could" *would* get me through the night.

Using the headlight for navigation was not as easy as I had hoped. It would barely illuminate the bank from the distance I needed to stay away from it. I had a much better chance in the middle of the river to keep from running aground or hitting a protruding boulder. I turned the light off and allowed my eyes to adjust to their widest light setting. I noticed black on either side of me and a barely noticeable dark sliver in front. This very slight color shading between black and almost black made all the difference in the world. "Follow the light shading of black; that's where the water is!"

When black got too close on either side, I moved away from it and centered myself as best as I could. The river had moved slowly all day long and now, in the darkest of night, it picked up. I found myself bouncing along in rapids, out of control. I prayed hard. I felt something bump from beneath. I had rolled over a boulder without damage to anything but my fear; it was soaring! I looked at my watch; it was 10:00 p.m. I had been on the river in the dark for an hour.

Once I was confused. "Where's the gray just lighter than black?" It wasn't in front of me. I reached for the knob on the headlight. I was headed for the rocky shore! I leaned as hard as I could and turned to miss the rocks just in time. "One prayer answered," I thought and reoriented myself to the lighter shade of black. I looked at my watch – it was 11 o'clock. I had been on the river 16 hours and two hours in pitch black. The river opened up wide as a lake. I wondered if I would ever find the opening where it would pull back down to a river. The lighter shade of black was all around me now. I began to despair ever getting to the bridge.

I remembered the launch was on the left of the river. So, oriented to the stars, I angled left and looked for the black on my left side. I found it and followed it for a mile or so, periodically checking with my headlight. I knew I was close, but the night was so illusive. I strained to see Shawn's bright light ahead, beaming me home.

A super-bright light shot across the water at me. "Shawn, is that you?" I called out. No answer. I repeated my plea several times, never an answer. "Lower your light! You're blinding me!" I yelled. No response.

Could it be a warning light on the bridge? I cut power, unable to see downstream in its blinding beam. Then, all of a sudden, a sign and a barbed wire fence appeared out of the black. The current dragged me right into the fence. I tried to push off, but the current had me trapped. I pushed again in a way to point my little craft upstream and pulled the throttle trigger all the way. Columbia slowly pulled away but not unscarred by the incident. The bright light went out. Night fishermen had irresponsibly not responded to my pleas or calls. I'm sure they were confused and not at all imagining the situation they put me in. I drifted past them, furious but not saying a word.

Just then a light shone down the bank. "Shawn, is that you?" I forgot the fishermen just yards away.

"Yeah!" He yelled back. "The boat ramp is down here!" His light bounced down the edge of the black as he trotted along and I followed a course just to the right of it. Between his light and mine, the image of a bridge came into immediate view. The whole nightmare occurred just 100 yards or so from camp. The fence out into the water was probably the rancher's campground boundary. I didn't care. I pulled Columbia up on the ramp sideways. We folded it up together, and he trotted off again along a dirt path while I puttered along at Columbia's slowest road pace behind.

I pulled off wet clothes, exhausted and ready to fall into bed. Shawn was excited. He'd made supper, so I ate it politely, trying hard to stay awake. I tried to forget the nightmare and regale to him the bigger part of the day, the beauty and fascination of the river. *Then* I fell into bed.

Seventeen hours and Pedal-Paddle Columbia had pulled me down 67 miles of the Upper Missouri Scenic and Wildlife River. The park service suggested these two sections of the river be done in four days. Just as 220 miles on land in one day proved Columbia's land ability, now no one can doubt Columbia's water ability, or that of "the little engine that could!"

DAY 11 – Short and Sweet

Needless to say, I slept late. I did get up and rudely woke Shawn as I hit the generator to revive the dying batteries with a quip. "Hey, Shawn. It's 6:00 a.m. If I start now I can make the last 60 miles!" He didn't even have to guess if I was joking. I fell back into bed and slept till 10:30. We woke to a howling wind that rocked the motor home.

Shawn cooked breakfast while I began writing "Day 10." We had a 14-mile and then 44-mile leg yet to do, and it had already been decided to split them up even though today meant only a 14-mile day. Fourteen miles was a joke for Columbia and me, but the weather outside was not. It was just like my first miserable day, but now I knew how to dress for it. I pulled on my suit while Shawn gassed up the bike, and we were headed for the launch ramp again, but not until more pictures from neighboring campers. As we prepared to launch so did two kayakers. "Wanna race?" they taunted. "Only if we run on land after we do water," I retorted with a grin. They got the point and slipped their perfect-for-this-environment steeds into the water after mine.

They were soon past me and leading the way. In their long, sleek, stealthy vessels, they cut through the water and the wind like a knife.

I followed as best as I could. We hit some rapids and I noticed they stopped at the bottom. I think they wanted to either catch their breath or see if I would make it, or just give them something to laugh at.

I did both. I let Columbia get sideways when the strong current and the whoop-dee-do's hit me. But I pulled it out, and Columbia's wide flat platform was almost as comfortable and stable sideways as it was going in front first. I rode the two-footers with ease and came out the other end with my competition already a quarter mile ahead. I chuckled at what they must have thought, watching Pedal Paddle bounce down through the rapids sideways.

They pulled out about seven miles down the river. I passed them and waved bye as they unloaded for a rest. I didn't rest in 17 hours yesterday, but then again the little engine did almost all the work. Did I tell you how much I love this little engine?

It began to rain lightly as I left them behind, and I laughed at myself for thinking, "Why are jets practicing so low in this area?" Then I had a second, more intelligent thought that it was the longest duration of thunder I could ever remember. It echoed on for 10 to 20 seconds!

I heard no more after that so I kept Pedal-Paddle Columbia headed down the river, determined to make the next seven miles even in a flood.

Instead of worse, it got better, much better. The wind slowed to an occasional puff. The canyon, with its purple striated walls, was beautiful, and it was all just for me to take in now. The river was running fast, and took a lot of attention, both in keeping Columbia straight and watching for protruding boulders or those sneaky ones that lurked just beneath the surface with no warning but a surface bubble flowing over the top.

I made several good calls and was swept past rolling water with just such a boulder looking up at me from underneath the water. Things were going by fast, but it was a great, short but sweet ride.

The "take out" point was easy to spot at the end of a long wide valley, a place where they were working on redoing the cable ferry system that had been in use in these parts for decades. The cables keep the barge from being swept down stream. The State of Montana pays someone to be on call 24/7. You drive up and telephone the attendant. Depending on which side of the river you're on, they either cross and load or load and cross, but either way you drive onto the cable barge. They float you and your car across the river and you drive off. An amazing system for these remote areas, and it's free to the public. You've gotta come see this area...*Very* unique!

Anyway, that was it. I pulled Columbia up on the shore, and there it sat until morning. It was only 4:00 p.m., and I beat Shawn to this spot, so I nosed around a bit. After the two men working on the cable ferry went home around five, I owned the whole canyon. Shawn showed up, we made camp and a campfire, and had a great dinner. We camped on the edge of this dead-end dirt road overlooking the river, 50 yards down hill. It was an unbelievably peaceful and beautiful setting and the weather was perfect. Low hanging clouds, not a breath of wind now, and a little time to just sit and chat as the fire burned and the sky slowly lost its already faint illumination.

You talk about dark, pitch black, no light. Down in the canyon with overcast sky, it was dark! But that was it. A simple, beautiful uneventful day, but I needed it. Yesterday, 17 hours and 67 miles of river, tomorrow the Dauphine Rapids! *See you tomorrow.*

DAY 12 — The Dauphine Rapids

The day's weather called for overcast and 20% chance of showers, the first I had heard in a long time. I was disappointed in that I wanted to strap the video camera onto Columbia's mast receptacle and video the rapids.

I had trained hard for just such a day, taking Pedal-Paddle out into the Gulf of Mexico into three-foot to four-foot waves and crashing surf, just to learn its balance in severe conditions. I was ready to "rock and roll," or roll over rocks, or something like that.

I started out in a light sprinkle. Dauphine Rapids was on the map as being in the first 10 miles of my 47-mile day. I hadn't gone a mile or two before the river turned fast. There was either no wind or a light wind at my back, a first for this trip. I bounced along in one foot to 18-inch rolls, keeping the nose headed down hill and prepared at all times for it to get nasty, applying power and shooting out a 30-foot tail of water when needed.

We bounced along for a mile, then two, then three in this same fashion — never at all drastic or out of control, but a fast, fun ride. I picked out the worst parts of the river rapids just to practice for "the big one." Four and five miles went by, then six. Sometimes a little faster, sometimes a little slower; a boulder to dodge now and then.

Then the river slowed again. The scenery was beautiful with the canyon getting deeper and deeper. It rolled along, very docile, for another mile or two until it slowly sank in… that was it! That was all there was to it? Nothing more?

I was a lot disappointed and a little upset. I went through the worst of every bad place in the river taunting and jeering, trying to pick a fight, but this section of the river was not a contentious woman but a lady, fair and sweet. Beauty was what she was about, not contest, and the canyon walls deepened and became ornate again. Not as ornate as the long trip of two days ago, but almost as breathtaking when you added the magnificence of sheer size to the equation.

A boat came pushing up the river about 25 miles down, the only boat I was to see all day. It looked official, and the two pilots didn't seem to be fishermen. I mused to myself that they either knew this river extremely well or hated propellers, one or the other, but I'm sure the former was true. Their eyes were on me as they passed by, but that was always the case. I waved and they waved back as they passed by in deep water 50 yards to my left. I hadn't gone more than a couple more miles when they passed again running downstream, looked me over again, waved again and continued on down.

Shawn had registered my descent at Coal Banks Landing, and I had discovered from two nights before at Judith Landing that Pedal-Paddle was the talk of the river. Many had already started to take note of our progress and how quickly we had descended the 150 miles of river. I suspected this craft had wandered up or been sent to check on me, in a nice and protective sort of way, and I appreciated both the effort and the gesture.

They were gone, and the river was mine once again. At one point, I started to pass a herd of cows with calves on the right bank. They must have heard I was from Texas, as they suddenly and simultaneously began to be "driven" by my little craft, always staying just a little ahead of me in a spirited walk. Mamas would nudge babies along to keep up with the drive.

As they came to a steep embankment that followed a cliff around for a half mile or so, I just knew they'd stop and turn back, but they single-filed the trail around water's edge, the back of the pack even now with me. I got to see, first hand, "up close and personal" the way a cow and her calf interact with one another as the drive continued. Fascinated by their behavior, we continued around the cliff to the next clearing, and a whole new pasture. I guess I had unknowingly done my job and they had done theirs. They moved away from the bank up into the brush, trees, and new grass, and the cattle drive was over. Great entertainment for 30 minutes of my day.

Later on, at about 40 miles, a rainstorm came up. As I heard the "jets" rip by overhead with their long blasts up and down the canyon, I pulled the small craft alongside the high bank of the river. I both considered and hoped the lightning would fry the hill 20 to 30 feet above my head before it would reach down lower and fry me. The rain came down hard for a while. I pulled, zipped and velcroed my parka and hood around me until I was wrapped up in my little cocoon all snug. I imagined I was an Eskimo, looking at the world through the arched door of his igloo as I peered out of the upper half circle opening of my parka hood.

It kept me well, and soon the rain and the thunder were gone. The river became glassy, and all was calm and perfectly quiet, with the sweet smell that only a shower of rain can leave. I breathed in deep through my nose and pulled the hood back to get more.

    I had been in the saddle now for 11 hours, figuring one more to go, with only one stop to empty a sluggish right pontoon. Like clockwork, I rounded the next bend and there was the bridge, 30 minutes early. I crossed under the bridge and slammed into a mile-long stretch of hard wind. Hitting the trigger, Columbia pushed hard. In minutes I was pulling her onto the dock sideways, and Shawn came running to help.

    By now the right pontoon had more water in it, so we lifted it and rotated it until water came running out in a steady stream. The rudder bracket on the top back edge of the pontoon was leaking. Now we knew what to do to stop the leaking, and put Columbia to bed for the night. Cooking and working on parts and maintenance for the next three hours, we finally fell into bed. My first water totals went through my head, 150 miles in four days. The park service suggests nine days for the trip. Take all of it or take some of it, but sometime in your lifetime, get to Montana and the Upper Missouri National Scenic and Wildlife River.

DAY 13 – Of Antelope and Rattlesnakes

This day we were back on the road again. I wasn't even out of the campground and we had our first actual mechanical malfunction. The "cassette," as it is called, the multiple gears on the rear wheel, would not engage. It just spinned free as I tried to pedal. We changed the back tire / wheel assembly out with the spare bike, and that took an hour with all the framework attachments. Then I was off, and the first thing I got to do was climb out of the river canyon heading north. This was equivalent to one of the mountain pass summits as the little engine and I did all we could together to make the climb. By the time we reached near level ground, I was soaked with sweat under my parka and pants in spite of the fact I had pulled out the liners.

I could now stop at a "snow chain removal" area and unzip everything. Seconds later I was rolling again. The wind was hard and gusty from my right, trying to blow me out into traffic. "Boulders in the water yesterday, diesel trucks today." I thought. "I'll take the boulders!" The scenery was less than spectacular but pleasant. The dry rolling hills sculpted the landscape while smaller individual mountain ranges were placed about on the various horizons.

I saw something move just a few feet ahead and caught the tail of a huge rattlesnake with my tires as it slithered off the road. I shivered at the feeling, and my imagination went wild with what-ifs. "Better me than Vicki," I mused, as my wife is deathly afraid of snakes.

I fought the wind so hard for the 70 miles to Malta, I can't say as I really got to enjoy much, but I did see two herds of antelope, more correctly "pronghorn," and have always been fascinated with these creatures. Did you know they're second only to the cheetah in speed, but unlike the cheetah can keep up their speed for literally tens of miles…I know at least 30! That's amazing.

Anyway, when we arrived at Malta to head east on Highway 2, my tire was low, so I aired it up. Within blocks it was flat, so we rolled into a local hamburger place where we ate and told our tale to the local newspaper. They were all very nice, and we changed our flat in their little picnic area and took off again. Four windy hours later, I had pedaled for most of 130 miles, fixed two bike problems, done a photo shoot and story for the newspaper and ducked into a rest stop for the night.

Not much to tell, but it all can't be exciting, I guess. Some days I just got 130 miles down the road and that's all I got. Tomorrow we get another half day of Highway 2 and then we're back on the Missouri River below Fort Peck Dam. *Can't wait! See you tomorrow!*

DAY 14 – Downhill Fast

When I awoke this day, we were in a roadside park 16 miles west of Glasgow. It was a beautiful day, light wind, not too cool. With my heavy orange suit, gloves and helmet, it was just right for the nice short ride to Glasgow. Shawn took off ahead of me, and shortly after I arrived. One of the most excited newspaper editors I had met to date bounded out of his vehicle. We immediately hit it off. I couldn't help liking him when his first comment, not knowing I was the inventor of the contraption, was, "That's the coolest thing I've ever seen!" He asked a ton of questions, and I answered them all with equal excitement and enthusiasm.

He was the first person it was genuinely hard to say goodbye to. I'm generally too driven and always antsy to get going. We made hasty farewells and I took off after brief instructions with Shawn.

When I got to the edge of town, the newspaper editor was there ahead of me, camera in hand, to memorialize my parting moments. I waved, gave a thumbs up, shouted thanks again as I whizzed by and kept on whizzin'.

They say the wind always blows in Montana, kind of like back home in the Texas Panhandle, but it was no more than pesky as I made the 30 miles east and south to the river behind the Fort Peck Dam.

There was some confusion, so I hailed a farmer in a small pickup who slowed to a stop to see what the stranger on the funny looking, two-wheeled thing might want.

I knew I was on the Fort Peck Indian reservation, but I didn't really expect to be talking face to face with this jolly older fellow who looked like he stepped out of the losing side of a John Wayne movie.

After giving me directions to a site to get on the river, he added, "You're not really going on the river with that thing, are you? They're lettin' a lot of water out of the reservoir right now, and mixed with last night's rain, that river's fightin' mad!"

I told him where we'd already been and that I'd be fine. He nodded and reminded me to "get back up on the oil."

"What's that? The oil?"

"Yeah, the black top…the pavement," he explained. I had never heard that term before and loved learning in such a fashion.

We both moved on as I thanked him once again, and soon we were "back on the oil" and briefly thereafter on the river.

The editor had warned me of some rapids "better than the ones on the scenic and wild upper Missouri," but I had no idea. I turned the very first bend and there they were. My heart jumped. This was the real thing. I was about to go downhill fast, and I knew it. I braced myself, lined up to the worst or best of it, depending on your view, and hit the throttle wide open.

I fell into the first hole and bounced out the other side, but not without both pontoons going completely under. I got out of shape and it was too late. I went sideways, and my left pontoon rolled down the slope into the next hole. I knew what was going to happen next. I scrambled to put my weight on the right pontoon and held my breath. The left pontoon went completely under at the bottom of the hole, and I felt the whole thing start to flip. I kept full throttle and leaned even harder right, the left pontoon reemerged out of the water and Pedal-Paddle Columbia throttled sideways to smoother water.

Undaunted and a little fierce, I pulled a right circle and went right back into the worst of it, determined to win. This time I hit the rapids head on, riding them out to the very end, bucking like a bronco front to back all the way but in perfect control this time.

Half of me said, "Yeah, that was great. This is what I trained for!" But, the other half said, "You could have gone around, stupid!" I decided the second half was just talking for Vicki since she wasn't there. I reminisced about my sweet victory over the rapids.

The river was fast; I felt it was much faster over all than the same river above Fort Peck Reservoir I had left only three days before. For the record, I attributed five miles per hour to this section of the river as there is no official map laying out speeds, distances, and river entries and exits as on the upper Missouri.

I swiftly passed peaceful stands of cottonwoods on one side with curved banks of dirt approximately 20 feet high on the other side. In fact, after the rapids, the next six hours teetered on peaceful and boring.

Every curve was low to the inside with a forest of

cottonwoods and high to the outside with a 20-foot bank of steep, steep dirt, almost a cliff. Curve after curve after curve after curve, always the same.

I would sometimes cut the engine with the wind at my back and just let the breeze and current carry me down that section. Or, I would cut the engine and pedal myself to keep the spray low as the back breeze would pick up the rooster tail and wet me and the engine with it. Other than this little exercise, the trip was very routine, until....

The river headed primarily east with long bends north and south. The roads are all on the north side of the snaking river so, of course, I had to be on the south bend when it hit.

A norther wind blasted in! As I rounded the corner to "S" back north, I came out of the protection of the trees to a mile-long stretch of "mad" wind and water. The current may have been "boilin' mad" but it could hold no candle to the wind. My little craft was nosed into two foot white caps in no time.

Without "the little engine that could," heading for shore would have been my only option. Pedal-Paddle Columbia's only real enemy was high wind on both land and water.

I hit the throttle wide open and began to drive head first into the waves. I bent over from the seat until my head was just above the handlebars to give the little engine a fighting chance. I sprayed water back 40 to 50 feet, carried by the howling wind. Columbia bucked as in the rapids before, with the two-footers hitting and rolling over her pontoons in quick succession.

It was a long hard fight for one mile, but that's how victories are won, in the trenches, one hard mile at a time. Without those long, hard miles, the next 200 easy ones couldn't be taken. So we hit, and we hit and we hammered, and we hammered one hour for one mile!

As the river started to bow east again, I spotted a low spot in the usually high cliff-like outer bend and headed for it. As I cleared to see down stream around the bend, there sat the chase vehicle just around the bend and 30 feet high on the ridge, a beautiful sight!

Shawn had played it just right, and came looking for me, knowing about where I'd be. I learned later he'd asked permission from the reservation farmer to be there, and seeing the trailer and RV parked high on the bank was like running from the Indians and seeing the fort on a distant hill, a bastion of security and shelter.

Seeing no other better way to exit the river than the one I was headed for, I kept hammering in that direction. The day had gone downhill fast, but the waves soon dropped to one foot and then zero as I approached the shore and high bank protecting me from it.

It was all Shawn and I could do to separate Columbia into the three pieces of bicycle, left pontoon, and right pontoon and haul them one piece at a time to the top of the embankment. We reassembled the craft quickly, and I started a long slow crawl over a quarter mile of irrigated farmland to get Pedal-Paddle back on the farmer's private dirt road.

Bad news had come via Shawn's study of the area. I now had to ride 20 more miles east in the wind to get to a suitable camp for the night. This would take me right up until dark. I was disgruntled, to say the least. I was tired, hungry, fed up and soaked right down to the socks and underwear with no time to do anything but ride 20 miles with a howling north wind at my left side.

I had just gotten back to the "oil" when a Native American couple whipped off in front of me, all excited. Now playing the part of "bad attitude boy," all I could think of was, "What now?"

"You're him! You're him!" they shouted, as they pushed a fresh newspaper in my face with a giant picture of me on the front page; taken just hours before! The excited couple insisted I take their paper, and I explained and showed how Pedal-Paddle works to show my gratitude. Needless to say, my attitude got immediately better, but I still had to ride 20 miles in wet underwear, so I thanked them again and took off.

The ride was just as miserable as I expected, but I was an instant local celebrity. As I went through the little town of Wolf Point, people waved and honked or just stood and stared in disbelief as the full page front cover picture of their little local newspaper came to life in front of them.

At one point, a pickup of excited teenage boys pulled alongside and all but begged for me to pull over and talk. Of course, I did, and then passed brochures all around. Their enthusiasm was contagious, and I made the last five miles with a smile on my face, but still wet down to the underwear!

DAY 15 — *Snow's* On the *Way* in Late *May*!

Today, at 6:30 p.m., actually ends two weeks of being on the road. It looks like I may have my first day to add no miles. The norther of yesterday evening blew in cold and overcast conditions, both of which I could deal with except the wind is *still* blowing out of the north.

We've made great progress. We've only added 400 miles this week, but 200 of these miles were water miles and that's big news. The trip has to be balanced to be truly amphibious. As I told the reporter yesterday, I can't say I did an amphibious run across America with 3,500 miles of land and 100 miles of water. At a four-to-one ratio, I'll still be on the water more than the land, but it's all about balance and being fair. These ratios and percentages have never been established for amphibious records. We hope to establish these and set several of these records before it's all over.

I've spent the morning writing Day 14 and looking out the window. As I sit here, I'm nothing less than elated at the trip so far. It has been an incredible journey with many successes. A sheriff is knocking on our door; I'll be right back....

I just talked with the sheriff. He came to check on us. He said snow was on the way. So...I'll forget the unpredictability of water egress and regress and take to land and get what I can. See you after a while....

I'm back, worn out and over 100 miles east of where I wrote that last line. The wind was hard out of the northeast, so hard, in fact, that I just pedaled harder than I have since the beginning of the trip.

The terrain was up and down all the way. I set the seat down as low as it would go to give me a low center of gravity and make a little less target for the wind, but it made me pedal hard with my knees bent.

Hard pedaling, knees bent, into a hard cold wind, up and down hills for over 100 miles. Hands freezing, body dripping in sweat. It kind of reminded me of how I feel at the end of a hard day of snow skiing, only this went on another four hours after I was already tired and my leg muscles were burning.

The gear pattern was the same over and over again with pedals churning fast; seventh gear, sixth gear, fifth gear, fourth gear, third gear, fourth gear, fifth gear, sixth gear, seventh gear and over again on the next hill. I wish I could say I enjoyed it, but this was a pure endurance run. I saw nothing but hard pedaling and pavement for six to seven hours.

I crossed over into North Dakota about 6:00 p.m. and into Williston about 7:00 p.m. That pushed our 2-week total to 1,500 miles; just 300 miles short of half way but way short on water miles. We may get 50 more miles of water before Bismarck which will give us 250 in the first half of the trip. I wasn't real concerned because I knew we'd get lots of water in the second half of the trip. We still had the Mississippi, Lake Michigan, Lake Erie, the Delaware River, the Hudson and New York Harbor.

Getting to Times Square by July 4th was my main goal, and getting in as much water as I could was my second. We should be okay. I was just a little disappointed that we went so far out of the way for 180 miles of water.

Anyway, we're here, we're okay, we're ahead of schedule on miles and although it's cold we're still moving, still getting news coverage, still getting people interested in Pedal-Paddle and still getting our pitch for a penny per mile for donation to CareNet, the charity we're riding for.

The motor home continued to give us more problems than the one-of-a-kind apparatus that was crossing America, and Shawn arrived one hour behind me into Williston. We traced the wire that was giving us no battery charge, jumpstarted the engine to charge all three of its batteries, let it run a while, and all was well. *We've changed time zones and it's 1:00 a.m. I have a 9:30 breakfast appointment with the local newspaper taking us to breakfast, so it's off to bed we go. What a day. Good night!*

DAY 16 – Pedaling to Survive!

I had made arrangements the evening before to have breakfast with the local newspaper sports editor. I had been told he was a Santa Claus look-alike and that's not an exaggeration. Fact is, he takes off November and December to be Santa Claus in Cincinnati, Ohio. Go figure.

When he pulled up to the motor home at 9:30, there was no mistaking who he was. An extremely pleasant fellow, of course. Shawn, Tom and I had a nice breakfast and talked of mostly Pedal-Paddle for well over an hour.

After asking our "flavor" of church, he dropped us off at a church he was sure we'd like and insisted on coming back to pick us up so he could see us off and take pictures.

We had a great morning, and church was a needed inspiration and encouragement. After changing into my heavy winter suit and helmet, I answered a few more questions, made my many thanks to the kind representative of Williston and took off. The last thing I saw of Williston was jolly old St. Nick, I mean Tom, snapping shots of me as I rode by waving and giving thumbs up.

The minute I left town the day went from heaven to hell, friend to foe, peace to war, with the elements. Right into a wind, stronger than the day before, I crossed the Muddy River Bridge to climb, climb, climb.

Neither of the Rocky Mountain passes could hold a candle to these conditions, uphill and into 30 mile per hour winds all at the same time. For the first time on this trip, I found out what first gear on this mountain bike was like. With the throttle pulled wide open and my legs spinning till they burned, I climbed the first hill at a speed slower than I *walk*! The only thing worse was when the road curved north or south and I would get a taste of the side wind. I've ridden Pedal-Paddle since the first one. In as tight a turn as I can pull off, I've never drug a pontoon, but it was now a concern while trying to track a straight line. Columbia leaned hard into the wind to find stability but there was none. I wove in and out of the right lane uncontrollably on the little farm-to-market North Dakota highway.

Shawn was left to overnight my daily writings back to the office and do laundry; a task sure to take at least three hours. There was absolutely nothing on the road until the first little village of New Town 75 miles away.

Determined to get out of the snow's reach by Monday, I pushed on as hard as I could, with nothing to do but go forward. I was between pain and disbelief as I shifted all the way down to first gear, hill after hill after hill.

Two hours and 20 miles later, I pulled off the road on a steep grade near the top, trying to find a place mostly blocked from the wind. I collapsed on my back on the slope off the road in the grass, trying to catch my breath. After a time I rolled over, got to my knees, and pulled some beef jerky and a water bottle from my bags. I searched for emergency energy supplements but they had not been replenished.

Except for an occasional car and an occasional farmhouse, there was nothing on this road. It's hard to understand this unless you have been in this part of the world, but Williston was the first place in a week and a half that our cell phones would dependably get any kind of signal at all! Tom had told me there are 600,000 people in the entire state.

So, I got back on the bike, started the engine and finished cresting the hill. At 25 miles out it started to rain, a freezing cold rain. The wind lessened just a bit, and I bent over and stopped pedaling just to give my legs a few minutes rest. They had been going hard for three hours now. My hands were starting to freeze and stiffen. My legs were even getting wet and cold, and I noticed they were beginning to show signs of slow, strained movement as well.

This was a new experience for me. My only memories even coming close to these sensations are of times at downhill skiing. I felt I had to move. Immediately my body was headed back in the right direction. My back was screaming to go upright but the wind was pitching me all over, and I was forced to pedal in this contorted position, just to maintain balance and keep from getting stiff. I began to exercise my fingers inside my gloves, just as I had done on the Idaho pass, and to switch throttle trigger fingers on a continual basis as well, just so they didn't freeze.

Thirty minutes of this torture was excruciating, an hour like a war movie prison camp. Two hours was indescribable.

It had been five hours since I left Williston, and I couldn't remember such torture in my lifetime. The cold, the aching joints and muscles, the back pain. Just when I was ready to give up and climb into a drainage pipe or something, the rain began to lessen.

With the shower now behind me, the wind shifted as well and pushed. Relative calm and balance were temporarily created.

I stopped pedaling and straightened my back for the first time in two hours. It was very mad at me but I just let my legs do the explaining; they had no choice.

I was amazed at how quickly the world became right again. Speed returned, relative warmth returned, different positions were now possible to stretch and relax every part of my twisted body.

At six hours, I looked in my little mirror and there was Shawn. I was almost upset that he was not there to see what I had just gone through, but I found a little solace in knowing he had to have gone through it as well, just behind me. Would it even be possible to explain, to relate in writing? I doubt it, but I've tried.

One more hour and we were in New Town, sitting, eating a hamburger and fries in the only place open, and confirming he had, in fact, waded through the same storm I had prevailed in. I felt sorry for him going through such a bad storm in the cozy comfort of the motor home. "I bet you had to stretch your arm out to turn on the wipers and turn the heat up, didn't ya?" I teased, but in the back of my mind I wouldn't wish my experience on anyone. "Pedaling for survival," I thought. Now that takes the prize. I'll never know for sure, but I'm convinced that I would have frozen to death or died of hypothermia if I hadn't kept on pedaling.

Now I shared the coziness with Shawn in our little box of toasty perfection and soft beds. We were 180 miles from where we were supposed to be snowed in. I wonder if it was worth it, but really, it's just one more tale to tell on this "Pedal-Paddle Across America" story. Who'd a thought snow would hit this late in the year? Montana turned out to live up to its reputation, scenic and *wild*, and North Dakota is both figuratively and realistically right beside it!

DAY 17 – A Dedication to Crosses

It's Monday morning, May 24, and what was supposed to hit as snow in Montana came down as a gentle rain all night and morning in central North Dakota. The locals needed this rain as they have been in a drought for years. Both Fort Peck reservoir and North Dakota's large lake on the upper Missouri, Lake Sakakawea, are way down.

Shawn and I were comparing state statistics this morning at breakfast. I thought a few repetitions would help readers in some parts of the world better understand the sparsity of population in this region of the United States.

I was born and raised in Amarillo, Texas, which is considered a mid-sized city by Texas standards. Montana is the fourth largest state in the U.S. Its largest city is half the size of Amarillo, and the entire state has approximately five times as many people as Amarillo.

North Dakota's largest city is similar with the entire state having only four times the population of Amarillo.

We are a country truly blessed with land and natural riches. Every American should thank God every day that we live in such a place of amazing abundance. The farms I've rolled by for hundreds of miles, and ranches too, are the envy of the planet. How rich we truly are.

Speaking of blessings, when I got up yesterday morning I had water dripping on my bed and clothes and had to place eight bowls and pans to catch the drips. I caulked the roof last night just before dark and this morning

I only have three. (Forgot to caulk the back window.) Anyway, it's nice Shawn did laundry yesterday, and I had a great sleep on dry sheets after a very tough and wet day yesterday.

The rain continued to come down. As soon as it broke, I planned to make a break for Cross Ranch State Park, approximately 100 miles, and set myself up for the 40 to 50 miles of river to Bismarck tomorrow. *See you after while....*

I'm back... It should have taken about six hours, but nine hours later at 8:30 p.m. I arrived at the rest stop, Lewis & Clark Interpretive Center, on Highway 83. It is 40 miles from Bismarck by road, at least 50 by water. We were just a mile or two from a boat launch here so we planned to stay the night and hit the water in the morning.

What took so long? Two – count 'em – two flat tires! I was so mad I could have spit nails. I planned two kind of "half days" to slow down a bit, but instead I've had two "hell days."

The six to seven hours I was on the bike were almost continual rain on the edge of being snow. So you can imagine what that was like. Actually, though, the wind wasn't so bad, and that made it pretty bearable.

Everything about this part of the world reminded me of just a little wetter "home." It was so similar to our home on Lake Meredith, it was uncanny. A dammed canyon lake with oil wells, cattle and some farming around...very much like home. It was nice but, because of its familiarity, it's not too inspiring to write about, but I saw something that was.

I dedicate this chapter, this day, to crosses. At 20 miles per hour you see and take in everything. How precious life is and how many precious lives have been lost on the highways where now a cross stands, sometimes alone, sometimes two or even three at a time. Once today, I saw a place with five crosses all lined up. Probably an entire family wiped out with only crosses remaining to mark the spot of their death. I wanted to cry as I passed the sight, overwhelmed by what must have been a tragic loss. I've seen too many crosses on this trip, literally hundreds.

It is my hope and my prayer that readers of this take note. Slow down; don't take chances, like passing on blind hills and all the foolish things I've seen. Can life be that fast paced that we have to take death-defying leaps to keep up? Every cross is a story, I'm sure, but I'm equally sure every person behind every cross would say, "The chance wasn't worth it." Most accidents don't just happen; they are created by taking chances.

I knew from this experience I'd come away a better driver. Slowing down a bit, giving more room to bicyclists or people stranded on the shoulder, and mostly, taking no chances!

There were other crosses I saw as I traveled, always three together with the one in the middle painted gold. There are a lot of religions in the world today, but only one has a risen savior, the one and only Son of God himself, sent to save us all, if we'll only believe this simple truth. It is so simple anyone can understand its simplicity, because you get it with your heart, not your head. Even I understand the simplicity of God's gospel. My heart has caught and believed this simple truth, and I hope you'll discover the simple truth of the cross in the middle, in your lifetime and on your journey. It's the best and most meaningful cross you'll ever find. This cross can change your eternity. Here's to that one all-important cross...Amen!

DAY 18 – If You Don't Quit, You Win!

You know the old saying, "Just when you think it can't get any worse, it does." Well, it did. I hate to sound like every day is a hard, tough, "barely survive" kind of day, but the last several days have been just that.

Today started out with Shawn's report, as I suited up, that the back tire had exploded to pieces in the trailer over night. I heard something but just thought it was a sound from the nearby highway.

When I stepped out, it was freezing cold outside, colder than the evening before by quite a bit. Later we found out the cold front had, in fact, made it further south and east than was expected and was fully upon us.

We scrambled to fix the flat, our third since yesterday afternoon, while I contemplated the cold at four miles per hour on water or the cold at 20 miles per hour on land. The media was geared up to catch me coming off the water right in downtown Bismarck, something we had been too remote to do before. Ever the camera hog and not wishing to disappoint, I chose the water.

Shawn fell down in the mud on the big motorcycle, and I had to climb the hill and leave Columbia by the water to help him lift it back to its wheels. He tied the gas can to the left pontoon support, took my helmet, and left for a day of fix-ups on just about everything in Bismarck, the largest city we'd seen in two weeks.

I hadn't gone a mile before the wind kicked up out of the north so hard I was having trouble controlling

Columbia. It kept wanting to turn into the wind, which was upstream. I would make it do a full circle and catch its downstream speed again and again.

Now, I've told you about Columbia's 20-foot rooster tail of water spray. Well, the wind — the ice-cold wind — was blowing it back on me. By the first three miles I was wet from head to toe, and by the first five miles I was drenched. Shawn and I had worked so hard to dry out my clothes from the night before, and they were already soaked. Water was even down in my gloves and boots.

The end result of all this wet clothing was that it lost its ability to insulate. I was cold and shivering all over. My hands especially were beginning to ache with cold again.

I figured out pretty quick my friend, "the little engine that could," was producing wonderful heat from its little exhaust exit, and I began immediately to utilize its heat, first on my right hand, then with a change of position, my left hand.

Wonderful, fabulous heat was blowing from my little friend onto my fingers as I cautiously kept them moving across the exhaust hole.

I kept this up for a couple of hours, all the while navigating the slow and thin waters of the Missouri. Downstream from Lake Sakakawea was noticeably less water than all I had experienced before.

A couple of times I thought I was trapped in water too shallow to float, but Columbia pulled itself over the sandbars with water so thin I had to balance my weight very carefully to get it to float free. Several times I had to get off and push it over the shallows, making sure my boots were totally soaked and full of water. I know of no other vehicle that could have done the job. The cold was so apparent my breath vaporized at every outward exhaust from my mouth. Winter weather had found me almost in June. A later news report said Alaska was warmer than this area of Montana and North Dakota.

At 14 of my 50 miles, I got a cell phone signal for the first time in two weeks. I called Shawn and told him I'd have to get out at only one third my goal, the last "out" before another after-dark exit from the water in Bismarck; something I just couldn't do. I found the boat ramp and took Columbia out, drained the pontoons and set it up for land travel.

He headed north and I headed south. We met in about an hour, north of Bismarck. I got my helmet and some dry gloves and sent him back to locate the nearest laundromat to start the dry-out process all over again. One freezing cold hour later, my back tire exploded in downtown Bismarck, four blocks from the laundromat!

I honestly was ready to throw in the towel. I had been chased by record-breaking cold, high winds, multiple motor home problems and now four flat tires in 24 hours!

The back tire not only blew, but tire and tube wrapped up the back wheel so badly it instantly locked down and went into a slide right in the middle of city traffic. Cars swerved to miss me, and then I had to literally drag it off the road. It took me 30 minutes just to unravel the tire-spaghetti from around the axle. Both tire and tube were totally destroyed and I was still cold and soaking wet.

After calling Shawn, I waited with the bike as he made his way back the four blocks and across traffic to get me. We loaded the bike, got to the laundromat and started the clothes drying while we changed the bike tire, rim and gears to the new ones Shawn came into town to get fixed.

While changing the back tire, I set the bike down on the *derailleur* and broke the *derailleur hanger*. The only one within hundreds of miles was on our back-up bike. We grabbed the clothes and headed for the bike shop.

Oh yeah, we discovered after almost completing a back tire change that the tires and tubes they mounted were the wrong size. So we had to go back to the bike shop and start all over again.

They changed the tires all right, and we gave them the wheel that kept popping so they could inspect it to see *why* it kept popping tires. They assured me they got it "whupped," and mounted both tires. I took the *derailleur* hanger off the bike in the trailer that was supposed to be "just like the other bike only last year's paint job," and the *derailleur* hanger was *not* the same." I found out they had a grinder and a hacksaw, so I went to work making modifications on it. I got it ready to go back on, but I asked the professionals to do it, as I had never replaced a *derailleur* hanger in my life. The "professional" proceeded to cross thread the bolt. I took it out, corrected it, got it to go in straight, and *that* was done.

We started to put the bike back together and needed an axle nut off the wheel that kept popping. They handed me the new fixed wheel, and I was threading off the axle nut we needed when it exploded in my face, right in the middle of the store. I was dazed and my ears were ringing, but otherwise I was all right. People are killed or seriously injured by stuff like that.

I kindly suggested that maybe it was still not quite right, and they went to work on it again, quite nervously I might add. I still didn't know if we could trust it but we paid our bill and left with two new tires on relined rims and with new sealant-proof technology.

Everything seemed fine. It was 6:00 p.m., with a media meeting scheduled at 7:00 p.m. with a TV station. I decided to try out Columbia before we loaded it. Everything was fine, but the throttle stuck wide open! It raced down the street in front of cars, but I was miraculously saved from harm again as I shut down the bike with the power off switch. Pedaling back to the trailer, I tweaked the throttle until I broke *it* as well. We had another engine, but I didn't have any more time.

We cleaned up, made our meeting with the local TV station, and then worked on taking the throttle cable assembly and carburetor throat out of the new engine and putting it on "the little engine that could." This took a couple more hours. It was now 11:00 p.m.

In the last 36 hours, I had five flats, one that blew up in my face. The freezing rain chased me for yet another miserable day, parts broke with wrong back-up parts that were supposed to fit, I had several other near death experiences from traffic, near hypothermia and who knew what else, with careless mistakes and incompetence all around me, including from myself, lifting and slopping a heavy street bike out of the mud, and running aground continually in record drought conditions in the river. When I said miserable, I meant miserable. Snow would have been welcome to what I've had for the last four days. Freezing rain doesn't mean little ice balls…I wish! I'm talking just above freezing, like 34-degree rain. I was wet, bone-chilling drenched all the way through, soggy, with no protection from my clothes. Pushing and pedaling for hours longer than my body should be able to bear and in all kinds of contorted positions, just to not be blown off the highway or out in front of traffic.

Bottom line… It was days like that and times like that when you either made it or you didn't. You either got it done or you didn't. You either picked yourself up and went on or you didn't.

And now we had a new spark plug and throttle cable assembly for "the little engine," a good tire and tube on the wheel that I had confidence in with new gears. My clothes were dried back out, the broken *derailleur* was working with the bracket I ground down to fit, and they said the freezing cold weather really was going away. I didn't know, but here's what I did know. Tomorrow we'll meet two TV stations and the newspaper folks at 9:30 a.m. I'll have a smile on my face, and a positive attitude again, and by 10:30 or 11:00 a.m. I'll be on the interstate headed east. It's what I *said* I was going to do. I had no choice. Winners don't quit and quitters don't win. If you don't quit, you win…*I've decided to win.*

DAY 19 – Riding the Wind!

I wanted to get a head start on the day, so I got up, cooked breakfast and had the bike in the water by 9:15 a.m. I wore a shorty wet suit, dive gloves, and dive boots; all for show, because I know they're not warm.

My plan was to get Pedal-Paddle up stream a quarter mile or so before the media got there so it didn't look bad going upstream so slowly. Columbia and the river's "fast side," which was the side the boat-dock was on, were a dead match for each other. I hit the throttle as I came around from the dock into the current and I was standing still, full blast and I was going nowhere. I pulled back to the dock, and a fisherman helped without asking. "The current's a lot slower on the other side," he said.

I thanked him for the advice and fought the current like a trout headed upstream until I had angled Columbia to the other side of the Missouri, 100 yards away. As I approached the other bank, Columbia moved more and more upstream until I had made the bridge a quarter of a mile up. "So this is how Lewis & Clark did it," I thought, as I contemplated what it took to paddle upstream. I looked across the river, and Shawn was yelling for me to come down.

The press had all gotten there while I was fighting my way upstream. I could hardly see them because they had set up their cameras in the bushes to get a sense of motion as I came by.

I put on a show for them, throwing a rooster tail and moving downstream quickly. I leaned into a perfect turn out of the current and in behind the little peninsula right into the protected boat ramp.

I made a few comments, then continued my show by folding Pedal-Paddle up on camera and flying away across the parking lot, doing a wide high speed turn, and running back right at the camera to a fast full stop.

One station politely conceded questioning for the other to go first. I answered their questions, bid them goodbye and turned my attention to the other station. They asked a few routine questions as the other crew packed up. The minute the first TV crew drove off, they exploded with previously contained excitement, asking me all sorts of questions as they circled with their big camera.

I was thrilled. At their begging I re-launched Pedal-Paddle for close up transformation shots and a re-launch and lap around the small, still, protected pool. They got a lot of great footage and I got a charge from their enthusiasm.

They waited while I changed into my bright orange road suit, got more footage and asked more questions. They taped even more as I drove off with a wave and a thumbs up.

My exit was great fun and lifted my spirits even higher. I cruised down the lush riverside road full of the morning's success and ready to try out my all-new rigged and ready Columbia. I felt sure all the bugs had been worked out and was ready for a lot of miles.

I had just passed the last exit for Bismarck when I heard a faint pop followed by a familiar "shew-shew-shew-shew-shew," the air leaving my tire as it turned.

I swerved to a stop in disbelief, looking down at my brand new $60 "best they had" tube and tire. Lifting one side with my knee and spinning the tire, I found a chunk of twisted, sharp steel about 1/4" wide and 1 inch long stuck into the tire. It was so large it looked hopeless. I had no can of "stop leak" as I depended on the "pre-slimed," puncture proof tube to get me down the road.

With no faith in what I was doing at all, I rolled the hole down, got out my little pump and pumped until I couldn't any more. It filled up then went right back down.

When I had regained my strength I tried again…same result. Again I pumped, and miraculously the huge hole healed itself! It held air!

I started to throw things back together, got on and took off. It was low on pressure and bumped as I rode. Looking back, I crossed the interstate, the grass, then the other side. I took the exit ramp and headed for the corner with the big fueling station.

Minutes later I had deflated, checked the tube for folds, re-inflated, tested and was off. I couldn't believe it!

I rode hard and long, not stopping for anything. After several hours I pulled off for fuel, left, and the bumping started again. This time it was my front tire, my first. It popped at just less than 1,800 miles, the official halfway point of my trip. An hour went by, and I started walking. I had walked about a mile when there came Shawn in the motor home with the trailer with everything I needed, including the one-mile ride back to where I had left Columbia beside the road. Being our first front tire flat, and much easier than the back, it was fixed in no time at all. I was back on my way. We rolled along keeping close, but lost each other when I missed a predetermined rendezvous at Wal-Mart.

It got cloudier and cloudier and became apparent I was on the edge of a squall line. The sky was black all behind me, and the wind kicked up in a rare "sheer wind" that was pushed from behind by falling rain.

It was right at my back. I couldn't imagine being wet and cold again, so I caught this "air wave" like a surfer. I rode it for all it was worth. It pushed me faster and faster until I knew I was going 40 miles per hour-plus on flat ground!

Once I kept up for a mile or so with a car on the access road. I was literally flying, gusts pushing slightly left, then right and on the edge of disaster the whole time. It lasted for miles, and it was getting dark. It was getting harder and harder to control the wild force coming from behind me.

I prayed for an exit with a restaurant, and there it was. Time to get off this wave. I cut the gas and coasted *up* the ramp so fast I had to brake. Think about it…brakes and uphill just to slow me down. I ran the stop sign after a good look both ways as the wind pushed me out into the intersection. I leaned hard to turn, still trying to slow down.

As the wind came into my left side, I leaned almost to the pavement with my left pontoon. The wind gusted and I feared being picked up and thrown over the rail to the interstate below. Now fighting the wind instead of being pushed by it, I slowed to less than a walk and kept all my weight on top of my new kite. It was barely under control, but I managed to hang on to it until I was able to turn again into the truck stop. I circled cautiously to the back of the building out of the wind and put Columbia to rest against the wall.

The town was Tower City, North Dakota. The folks were friendly, helpful and nice, and the food was great. Afterwards I asked the price of a shower and took them up on their offer of "free."

Shawn rolled in later that night on dead batteries. The RV died in the parking lot, so we did, too. Even with two flat tires, we had made 160 miles and TV news to boot. It had been an exciting and rewarding day!

DAY 20 – Kicked Off the Interstate

I had 40 miles to make to get to Fargo, North Dakota, and after that the Minnesota state line. I had TV crews to meet around noon, so I headed out. The weather was nice, but the roads were terrible. Construction most of the way forced traffic into a single lane, with only cones between them and one of the worst interstate shoulders I had seen. It was thin, chunky pavement, with bad dip lines and strings of grass growing through. It shook and bounced Columbia and me miserably. Every pothole transferred directly to my lower back, and they were frequent.

Diesel trucks flew past me just three to four feet off my left side. As luck would have it, a truck pulling a crane marked "wide load" squeezed past me just two feet off my helmet. At that distance, the crane itself had to have passed over my left pontoon. It was probably one of the worst overweight, oversized loads I've ever seen go down the highway. It had 12 support axles with four tires each and two steering axles for a total of 50 tires on the ground! Compare that to an 18-wheeler! It was all over so fast I didn't have time to get scared. I just shook as I saw it roll off ahead of me.

I arrived in Fargo with TV cameras set up on the highway to catch my arrival. Very flattering, so I waved, gave thumbs up and passed them by full throttle, which was what I thought they would want me to do. Then I took the next exit into a truck stop to answer questions.

Very nice local news folks introduced themselves as they hooked me up in the usual fashion with a clip-on mic and transmitter pack attached out of sight. I answered their standard questions and rambled a bit on the ones they missed that everyone else wanted to know.

They informed me that they passed my chase vehicle stranded on an on-ramp a couple miles back and we said our goodbyes. I called to find that Shawn had once again called and was, once again, waiting on a tow truck.

Another TV station was a "maybe" for after four o'clock. A full five hour wait for a "maybe" in the middle of my day, my best time to move, was judged "unreasonable" by me so I hit the road to make whatever miles I could towards Minneapolis-St. Paul.

After the terrible road conditions leaving North Dakota, I was just settling into one of the best situations I had driven on, a broad new concrete highway with a shoulder as nice as the two lanes of traffic themselves…a first in the entire trip. I hadn't gone five miles out of the city when I heard a funny sound from behind. Looking in my rearview mirror, I had a black official SUV looking vehicle on my tail.

I came to a stop, and a very pleasant officer firmly informed me there was a 40 miles per hour minimum speed limit on Minnesota interstates. I was braced for this to happen at some point. There was no getting around it. I was directed to U.S. 10, a four lane that paralleled the interstate. I was a little upset as I pedaled north to U.S. 10 to find conditions exactly like I had left in North Dakota, with traffic stopping in every town and worse pavement again. I was made to go from a safer, more relaxed condition to a situation where traffic moved just as fast, was more crowded and road shoulders were so bad I had to weave up onto the lanes of traffic at every opportunity. It was a dangerous situation, but it kept Columbia from getting beaten to death.

Lest you think I exaggerate, within 30 miles I was broken down on the side of the road, not with just a flat, but a broken rim as well with only the untrusted spare left in the trailer five hours away, and a new one 150 miles and two days ahead, at best.

Let me just stop here and say this. America needs exercise…desperately. And America needs to be more conscious of fuel efficiency. Neither of which can happen with bicycles when we make no room for them. After 2,000 miles, I'm appalled to see lanes for cars and trucks having springs, shocks, and air ride that are swept clean of debris while bicycles, mostly without all these same comforts, are forced to ride on rough, bumpy, hardly ride-able shoulders, all the while dodging the debris swept to them from the other traffic lanes. Take a good, slow, hard look at the shoulder, if there even is one, of most roadways in America and you would be appalled. Making a better place to ride for those trying to save fuel and get exercise just makes good sense, and America needs to make some changes.

A change in the attitude and awareness of motorists should be a priority as well, with much more courtesy to bicyclists trained into the education of our drivers. I'll take a guess that not one question on one test in any one of the states' driving exams relates anything at all to courtesy or safety regarding driving in the presence of bicyclists. The average driver certainly doesn't drive as though they've even considered what might be important, needful or even safe for bicycling the shoulders of our highways. The professional truck drivers, I must say, have been very good to me, almost always moving over a lane when they could to provide an extra margin of safety and being responsible with their wind turbulence. Those driving motor homes or pulling trailers, in contrast, almost never do that. It's time for some change.

Oh well, off my soapbox and back to my story. That pretty well finished off my day. I sat in a gas station and then a restaurant to pass the time. I did get to see myself at five o'clock on the news for the first time since we left, a fun treat for me and those in the little neighborhood, highway corner restaurant.

One of the customers, a nice retirement age lady, gave me a ride back to my fallen steed. Shawn showed up an hour and a half before dark. We changed out the rear wheel assembly and I got 30 more miles. One hundred miles and TV news spots; not bad for having my best five hours to get down the highway destroyed, but still frustrating for what it could have been. We ended out the day with still more motor home problems but brought it to rest at a really nice rest stop for the night. *Tomorrow we'll see what kind of job the bike shop did on our untrustworthy backup wheel assembly. I'm going to bed with a little faith in it. I did make it the last 30 miles and felt pretty good. Special thanks to a couple of really nice truckers who helped us isolate the RV's problem and get it parked. Life on the road seems to keep repeating itself, crazy situations, great people. See you tomorrow.*

DAY 21 – Back to "Almost" Normal

I said goodbye to the rest stop quickly this morning. I downed a bowl of cereal and dressed while Shawn readied my gallant steed and I was off. The bike felt good, the weather was good, with just a mild headwind, and the countryside was especially pleasant.

I passed farm after beautiful farm. The whole countryside was so well taken care of. I was very impressed. I saw turkey farms, chicken farms, pig farms, dairy farms, grain silos of every shape and size: an amazingly abundant, fruitful and green land. All varieties of trees, in groups together, were left in the original, natural state. Streams, ponds and small lakes were everywhere.

I fell in love with Minnesota as I rolled along, my first time ever here. My travels had taken me to all but two of the 48 mainland states, and North Dakota and Minnesota were the two that had somehow eluded me. There were "watch for snowmobile" warning signs quite often along the highway, reminding me that this part of the country is not always so pleasant, but today is the first mild day I've seen in weeks, and was just too pleasant to think of anything else. I was glad now to be "kicked off" of I-94, as the US 10 Highway is now much improved and has a wide, smooth shoulder. I glided along easily but got to see more of the countryside as the highway slowed and narrowed in each town, usually to a single traffic light, and moved on again.

All in all, it was a very uneventful day, something I desperately needed. The headwind was enough to keep me pedaling uphill only. There weren't too many hills and none all that steep. I think I switched down to sixth gear one time.

People in Minnesota were very enthusiastic about Pedal-Paddle. At every gas stop a group of people would ask about the contraption and the trip. More than once I heard from a passing car, "Hey, cool," or something similar. Once a couple pulled over in front of me and motioned for me to slow to a stop so they could ask the usual hundred and one questions, a very nice and excited couple.

I passed a "water sports" specialty sales yard and couldn't stand it. I turned back just to show them Pedal-Paddle, and they immediately bought some for their business. I don't know how many because I handed the phone over to Patrick, our manager in Texas, and waved goodbye as they talked. This scenario was supposed to have been repeated over and over again by Shawn and the chase vehicle, setting up dealerships as we went, but Shawn had spent the whole first half of the trip working on the motor home, and this objective of the "Pedal-Paddle Across America" had gone almost 100% undone. Although this is not what this book and my part of this trip was about, it was always in the back of my head and always driving me crazy to see one of our four major objectives to be so totally ignored and thrown to the wayside. I'm glad I stopped. It was a short, pleasant side trip with great, positive results. "This 'land of 10,000 lakes' needs two Pedal-Paddles on every lake," I thought, as I rolled along. It was just too perfect here for these water toys, and the relatively flat terrain would make it easy to get to the water on the regular human-powered version.

All in all, I rolled along for eleven hours. I stopped a little more often than usual to report my position for two reasons. One, Shawn was still back where I left him, working on a fuel pump for the motor home. Two, it was so darn convenient.

I had been told I had six news channels interested in doing a story on Pedal-Paddle Across America so I pushed on until almost dark. Then I called Shawn to find out nothing had actually been set up. I was a little disgusted but still glad I had pushed 160 – 180 miles out of the bike that day and that it had rolled along without anything more than some adjustments.

I stopped 30 to 40 miles out of the Twin Cities, an easy reach for the morning news connections. I had a great meal at a local restaurant and then went and got a less-than-great room, although cheap, at the only local motel. I called Shawn to discover simple fixes to the RV had been unsuccessful and a decision was made to tow it back to Fargo, North Dakota, instead of forward to St. Cloud, Minnesota, towns of equal size and distance. I didn't know why, I just knew it was a motel for me and that was fine. A hot shower and some time to myself were well worth the forty dollars.

Rain was in the forecast for tonight and tomorrow. Vicki was on her way to meet me after 2 1/2 weeks. I wished she were here now. It looked like good weather to just hide out for a couple of days. We'll see.

DAYS 22 and 23 — A Short Day and a Day Off!

Well, I just called Vicki and Shawn. Shawn, no answer. Vicki, just six hours away! I decided to get a hot shower, then ride in the cold rain. I didn't have the liner in my parka. I'll find a motel and some clothes down the road closer to Minneapolis – St. Paul. See ya later....

I'm back. I made 20 miles in the blowing rain, blowing right at me, of course. I stopped for a McDonald's, my first in forever, booked a local motel (much nicer), went by K-Mart for a few essentials and there I was. I spent an hour drying out and watching this funny little box in my room they call a TV.

Hot bath, shave, brush teeth, wait for Vicki. That was pretty much it for today, and I'll probably take day 23 off. From looking in the mirror, I'd say I lost about 10 pounds in two weeks, just for anyone who might be considering a "bicycle diet." I'm sure exercise is the best diet there is. See you in a day or two. I've been 2,000 miles, and a day off sounds really good…!

"Thanks, I needed that," as the old commercial goes. We had a great time. We spent most of the rainy Sunday at the "Mall of the Americas" just south of Minneapolis, but on the way, we went by to see the Corps of Engineers Lock No. One. It was fascinating. We got a special tour by the nicest guy. We told him what we were doing, and he got genuinely excited. He showed us all about how the locks work and then told us all we needed to know to lock down the Mississippi River. The locks are huge, but he made it all seem so simple and routine that it took away my fear and apprehension. "It's all done by valves," he said. "You just open valves and let millions of gallons of water flow into the lock. Then you open another valve and let millions of gallons flow out of the lock." The gates, we were told, open and shut by hydraulics. Still, it was so big, it was hard to imagine my little 7'10" vessel down in there, but soon we would find out!

The overcast morning was turning to rain so we thanked our guide and got instructions to the mall. We twisted through beautiful, wooded, riverside streets and then popped up on the interstate for a few miles, and we were there.

We spent eight or nine hours at the "Mall Of the Americas."

It was a great day. I know this has nothing to do with "Pedal-Paddle Across America," but I especially loved the huge five-acre open area in the center with the "Camp Snoopy" amusement park and "Lego Land" attraction. Watching the kids at play just did something for my spirits.

Vicki and I had lunch at a favorite old chain restaurant we hadn't seen in years, walked around the five-acre center twice and ate dinner at a Hawaiian theme restaurant. I think I gained back the 10 pounds I lost in one day. It was just good to be inside, out of the weather, in total man-made bliss, after all the nature and roughness.

Not much to tell really. A typical goof-off day at the mall, so let's get back to the trip.

DAY 24 – Coming Back Easy, by Accident

I planned a huge and heavy day, 40 to 50 miles from north of the Twin Cities to south, outside the southern loop. I had been told by an officer of the lock and dam system that the river was high and running at four knots. Columbia would add three knots to my speed, so I calculated the distance as best as I could. Seeing as how the first half of my day's trip was above the charted navigation areas, I felt six miles per hour would be a conservative estimate of speed.

When I left the motel, I went backwards seven miles west because I wanted to see the Mississippi transform from a meandering, primitive, 100-yard-wide, natural river to the deep controlled "concrete jungle" of the Twin Cities. It was an incredible experience. I started out passing farms, parks and occasional houses. The houses appeared more and more frequently until they were side-by-side lots. Islands of every size and shape were commonplace and always deeply wooded.

Hardly an island went by without signs of children and teenagers claiming them as theirs for the summer, evidenced by swinging ropes and paths heavily trodden. "This would be a fun place to grow up," I thought.

I love the zeal of the Minnesota people for the outdoors. On the Friday before, all roads leading out of the city were jam packed with every type of recreational product imaginable. This area of four distinct seasons had an obvious gusto for summer and water activities, and it showed.

I could hardly go 100 yards down the river without a hearty shout, thumbs up, wave of interest, or someone out and out stopping me to talk about my journey and my contraption. It was very refreshing to see even children and teenagers with such an interest and zest for the outdoors. They really take advantage of the "10,000 lakes" they've been blessed with.

As I came further down the river toward Coon Rapids, the scenery became less attractive to me personally. A dam at Coon Rapids had changed the mighty Mississippi into an obvious residential-lot selling venture, with nice homes, jet skis, and boats of all sizes ripping up and down the long, skinny lake, a far cry from the natural unspoiled beauty and serenity I had enjoyed just a few miles behind. The weather changed as well. The sky blackened and began to pour out buckets of water on the already abundantly watered terrain. I pulled over my poncho and rubber gloves and enjoyed the fact that it temporarily chased all the "wake makers" away.

The shower was short lived, and about the time it slowed to a stop the warning signs for the low dam began to appear. I followed the warnings to move left and exited the lake near the left side of the dam. With a few brief directions from a friendly local lady and her son, I folded up Columbia, throttled it around the dam on paved paths and went in search of a re-entry point, just as canoes would do.

I followed the bicycle path to a small bridge that came down low to the water and began to scale the small embankment to the river. Hiding from the rain under the bridge was a family of puzzled looking fishermen of all sizes, a family of six. "You're not going to believe what you're about to see," I teased. Then folding Pedal-Paddle back out, I flipped the switch and pulled the cord to a polite idle of "the little engine." As I pushed out, all those under the bridge forgot the rain and ran out to the place I had just left. It was filled with loud and excited admirers. I shouted back my over 2,000 miles stats and they cheered me on as I waved goodbye to the brief encounter.

The river was back to "au natural," and I loved the islands and parks with an occasional home that mostly looked perfectly cared for and, well…perfect! Like a painting was every setting, each in a different style or tradition.

My estimations for the day were so far off, it was unbelievable. I hadn't gone half as far as I thought I would and called Vicki for a take-out point north of the city at Loop 694. It was the last boat dock before going through the city, and there was not another take-out point on my map until the southern loop, 40 to 50 miles further down.

The journey soon ended with the sighting of Loop 694. I moved left after the bridge and made my way to the waiting boat ramp. It had been a great day, although only half the water I intended to cover. *I dream of tomorrow with the news coming out, going right through both downtowns, and "locking through" for my first time ever. See you there!*

Day 25 – Locking Through!

I've been looking forward to this day ever since the State of Texas made me legally register Pedal-Paddle Columbia because it had a two-hp bicycle motor on it, and that made it a motorboat. You've got to be asking yourself, "What's that got to do with anything?" Well, I found out that any legal, registered boat, no matter what size or configuration, must be locked through the locks and dam system on any U.S. river...law! And today is the day!

It started out fairly normally with a two-mile land ride back down to the river from the motel. Try this in your canoe or boat. I had scouted a place to launch so as not to have to get back on the interstate bridge and cross the river to the public boat ramp. It was a secluded fishing spot just off a public park bike trail.

I folded out Columbia and slipped into the water. The dependable "little engine" went from a purr to a whirr, and we were off. The scenery was just as I had left it the afternoon before, but that was all about to change...drastically.

Both sides of the river were public parks for quite a while, and then I came under a bridge and ran "smack dab" into industrial-sized river shipping. Barges dotted the shores, either filled or being filled with grain, coal, sand or gravel from piles several stories high or from elevators.

Factories, storage facilities, power plants all lined the shores. Workers ran to grab cameras, as I was the oddity in this setting. No matter how strange my surroundings were to this West Texas boy, my surroundings were purely mundane and routine to the people who worked here. Grown men came running, as if they walked around with cameras in their hands all day, to wave so I'd wave back and they could get a shot of me, no doubt for the unbelieving wife and kids that evening.

I loved Minnesota's enthusiasm for Pedal-Paddle. The people there rekindled within me the knowledge that Pedal-Paddle really is cool and being outside and on the water is really a desirable thing. I was impressed with this state's natural beauty and the sincere warm and friendly nature of its inhabitants.

Industry gave way to commerce as the skyscrapers of Minneapolis loomed overhead. Parks still frequented the river shore and I can't say as I've ever enjoyed coming into a city as pleasurably and comfortably in all my life.

I felt so welcome as I approached the first lock. It was flashing green for me to "come on in!" I just knew Vicki and the press must be waiting on me. It was all so perfect, and they seemed so prepared for my arrival.

I hadn't seen a single tug or barge in motion all morning, so when a blast came from behind me a quarter mile, I jumped out of my skin. Very much shaken, a little embarrassed and with great urgency, I turned Columbia sharply right and raced for the side. The barge with its mass of steel just cleared behind me.

I waved at the man standing on the front of the barge, and he waved back as he passed by. I waved to the captain, high in his two-story pilot seat, but he just motioned for me to stay to the side and out of "the lane." I took my rebuke; glad it didn't have a worse consequence. I could have been killed!

The barge took what I thought was my place in the lock, and I sheepishly looked for the pull rope on the side of the entrance that signaled I wished to be locked down, while my heart searched for its normal rate.

A young but authoritative voice came over the speaker. "You want to lock down?" he asked.

"Yes sir...please." I said, as though I was talking to the "Wizard of Oz."

"Is that a registered vessel?" came back the voice with the question I longed to hear. "Yes, sir," I perked. "TX-8508-PX!"

"It'll be 20 minutes while I let down this barge and bring the water back up," he said with a slight apology.

"Thanks, or thank you," I corrected myself nervously, and all was silent.

I waited at the signal rope, hanging onto the wall until my own appointment with "the great and powerful wizard" of the magical lock. Finally the lights blinked yellow. I scrambled to fire the "little engine" and pulled a U-turn in the current to head down the "corridor with no ceiling."

As I approached, the giant gate swung wide and I gained admittance into the inner chamber, the Holy Grail, if you will. My awe of the whole thing was shattered when friendly faces with waving hands met me inside *with a camera*! I was in shock. Once again, the extraordinary, exciting and massive fell to the knees of the little, fragile and curious. I took a long, heavy rope from one of the men as they and a blonde lady, also in uniform, asked questions and apologized for not seeing me, "I was so small." I pondered the need for such a long rope but never asked.

"You're about to be at the bottom of a very deep hole," the lady said. Suddenly the length of the rope made a little more sense. "This is the deepest lock on the Mississippi," she reported, "We're about to let you down 50 feet."

I looked at the rope and yelled, "Wow!"

"Yeah, wow," she said. And I began to drop and drop and drop.

When it was all over, I was in a huge concrete and steel pit approximately 500 feet long by 75 feet wide and 50 feet deep! I looked like a minnow in a bathtub if even that big. She promised to send the digital pictures to our website, and the vast steel doors were opened to a waiting river at my new height. I looked back at the vast steel doors, leaking as they held back a 50-foot high wall of raging river, and I shook at the thought as I purred my little craft out the other end with a wave and a "thank you" to those who had done me this service.

I knew there was another municipal lock but I couldn't believe it was immediate. This lock, radioed by the other, was waiting for me with flashing green lights. This time the lights were mine and I sped right into the chute. I was a pro at this now, having done it one whole time before, and with the same questions complete with pictures, I was ready to leave when someone yelled down into the hole, "Wait just a minute, your wife is here and wants to get a picture." I thought it must be her and the news people, but no, it was just her. "My God!" she exclaimed as she leaned over the rail and saw where I was.

"You should have seen that one!" I yelled back pointing just up stream. "It's twice as deep as this one." With that I posed, waved, and pulled out onto the turbulent water as it merged with the still water of the chamber.

Minneapolis is a beautiful city with parks all along the river for miles. I looked over my shoulder often, not wishing to repeat the same mistake with the barge. They move up the river slowly but down very quickly, and you can't forget that. With high, wooded hills on either side, I couldn't believe I was even in a city. The only signs of city life existed in the frequent high bridges overhead with traffic congestion or the many people enjoying the park's trails that followed the shores.

I was so swept away by its beauty, the next six miles to the "U.S. Corps of Engineers Lock and Dam #1" seemed like no time at all. Vicki and I had visited this facility the morning of our day off, so it was very familiar to me. I looked to the rail on the right as I approached, and there was Vicki and the cameras. As I approached I waved at the TV camera pointed my direction with an operator behind. I was getting good at figuring out when I was "on camera" and when I was "off."

Bill, our tour guide, was working today, and he had everything set up for us. He ushered the cameraman around to the best views and was just great. "How'd that blonde at the first lock treat ya?" he yelled.

"Great!" I reported. "She took a lot of pictures!"

"That's my better half," he shouted, and a few more pieces to the day's puzzle made more sense.

"Very nice!" I shouted back and with a repeat performance down to 38 feet, I fired up, waved, yelled "thanks" again and was off.

It started to rain as I left and got really hard really quick. It had sprinkled on and off all day but now was coming down really good. Except for a couple of marinas and a bend in the river with several apartment buildings looking down on the water, things stayed pretty much the same.

At one point, another stream or small river merged with the Mississippi. From that point on, logs, branches and debris floated in chains down the river. Sometimes two and three trees were caught together and floating. All in all, it was a lot to have to dodge, but Pedal-Paddle's protected paddles were once again perfect for the job and got me through it all without incident.

Having heard the term "Dallas-Fort Worth Metroplex" all my life brought another "Wow!" to my day. You see, I thought "Dallas" in the term got top billing because it was larger; it never dawned on me it simply came first alphabetically. Thus the term "Minneapolis-St. Paul" metroplex held the same meaning. That is, until I turned a bend in the river and saw St. Paul. Wow!

Something about the way it sits on the outside bend of the river magnifies its skyline, and what a skyline. A very modern and beautiful city, it is much more visible from the river than Minneapolis. I buzzed along its busy shores, with roads and highways right down by the river. Tourist steamboats were parked everywhere, getting ready for the summer season. The whole city seemed ready to explode into summer, and its character was totally different from its "twin."

Barges, too, were stacked three and four wide on its shores, waiting to go up or down, parked neatly and in rows to the side of the river. In reverse, cosmopolitan turned to industrial, and piles and elevators of all types of commodities lined the shores behind waiting barges, with only parking space for the one being loaded or unloaded.

This common denominator never stopped until I-494 and a waving Vicki pulled me across the river from the abandoned boat ramp on our map to a new one on the opposite side of the river. It took all of Columbia's power to switch sides and not lose ground against the current, but once again "the little engine that could" did not fail me and I pulled Columbia up on shore an estimated 42 miles downstream from where I had started. Our motel, she reported, was only one mile away.

DAY 26 – All About Water Miles

As of today, I have 2,280 miles, approximately 280 of which are on water. Just two days ago only a little over 200 miles were water. It's time to equalize the numbers a bit. I need to see 400-plus miles on water before I leave the Mississippi to even have a chance at 1,000 miles on water for the trip.

I was out the door at 6:00 a.m. and on the water by 6:30. As I launched Columbia and hit the throttle, I immediately spooked two deer I had not seen before just downstream from the boat ramp. They jumped up the embankment then turned to look and just stood there, staring as I whirred on down stream. Again, it seemed their curiosity outweighed the urge to run, and I got a good look at two beautiful animals in the early morning light.

The weatherman predicted a north wind, perfect for my southeast trek, but the wind fooled us all again and blew out of…you guessed it, the east again. It was not hard, though, and except for a few bends in the river it was a great day even with the wind.

The industry seemed to flow down river with the water, and barges lined the shores in many places. The river and its valley were a little wider now, and an occasional marina hid back behind the trees with only its small inlet and a few boats visible from the river.

Interesting things stood out to this West Texas boy, like the railroad bridge which, when a barge came up river, pivoted from the middle. I guess a 100-foot span on either side swung around, making two big holes for the barge to pass through. Apparently one could pass on one side while another passed by on the other side. It was quite a sight for me to see the whole operation from start to finish, another perk of being so slow, I suppose.

I locked through Corps of Engineers Lock No. Two with a little difficulty. I thought the pull rope was at the end of the concrete pier and hated how stupid I must have looked as I searched for it. It was surprisingly close to the gate. I pulled the rope. No one spoke to me or acknowledged in any way I was there. Some 10 to 15 minutes went by, without so much as a little noticeable activity on the sides and my end of the lock. Then the lights began to flash yellow. A few minutes later the gates began to open to an empty chamber. I waited and as soon as the gates were fully back the light flashed green. I looked back to see if it was really for me. No one or nothing was there, so I took a leap of faith and just motored through the opening.

Once inside and the workers saw my craft, everything changed, like a seemingly shy child that decides you're suddenly all right to talk to and begins to chatter continuously.

I answered all their questions and exchanged pleasantries, and the gate opened and I was now down one foot from where I started! A huge difference from the 50-foot deep chamber of my first "lock through." I motored out, waved goodbye and was off.

Back on the river again, I began to see all types of trees. Little towns passed by from time to time. By Lock No.

Three I was a pro. For my fifth lock, I buzzed right up to the rope, pulled it, went in quickly, answered all the usual questions, and was out the other side before I knew it. There were boats everywhere after this lock with Lake Pipen just down stream. I was out of gas and soon to be out of sun. I enjoyed the little fishing boats and vacation houses, usually perched on piers, as I made my way to the docks of Red Wing, MN.

Red Wing is a river town all the way, with marinas, river commerce, and loading and unloading docks for barges. A not-so-little town, it covered the hills with buildings of all sizes and shapes. It is a great looking community.

I had logged 11 hours on the river, and that was enough. I knew the next 20 to 30 miles would be slow without river current to speed me along, so I met with Vicki and told her of my plan to bypass the long lake for a faster option down stream.

Columbia took to the highway for two hours without complaint. The vistas of the lake from the highway were nothing less than spectacular. The brown waters of the Mississippi turned a deep blue in the lake, and pleasure boats and fishing boats were everywhere. I recognized a few of them as boats that had sped south on the river past me earlier that day. I thought how neat it was that all of this water was so connected. You can go from Minneapolis to New Orleans, or Cincinnati or beyond, visiting places like this as you go. I was amazed at the thought of it all.

I pulled into the parking lot of our little motel for the night. "What a life," I thought. The river life! Such freedom, such opportunity, such adventure. I couldn't get it out of my mind. How connected most of the world is by water! *It sends me daydreaming even as I write this.*

Day 27—The Lock System Fails Me

I got up at 6:00 a.m. for an early shot at the river, but I let Vicki talk me into a "sit down" breakfast. It was a nostalgic old cafe. A storefront out of a long line of storefronts on an old brick block of storefronts...the way towns used to be...you know, Main Street, small town America. We were in Winona, MN, the town "Grumpy Old Men" was filmed in, so if you've seen the movie you've seen what I'm talking about.

We had a great breakfast and I enjoyed just being "one of the gang" with the locals at the old eatery. The fishing shop next door had caught my eye, or maybe it was my feet that got caught. They had been wet for days and I spied a pair of tall rubber boots in the window, the kind grumpy old men like me like to wear. So after breakfast I went in and bought the boots. My feet loved me for it.

We got some bad information and it caused us to get to the water at 9:00 a.m., a situation that would cause me great pain later on.

I paddled about an hour to the first lock and was surprised to find it was down river from the lake. I thought I had gotten on the river below the dam because the mile wide lake we enjoyed the evening before was down to just 100 yards wide or so. The lake is a natural depression and the dam is just there for control.

I rolled along enjoying the day. It was beautiful weather, warm with light winds, with one little village after another. I wanted to come and live in every one I saw.

The road overlooked the river, sometimes for miles. I enjoyed just watching the cars and trucks pass by, and was glad that I was not one of them. I was expecting Vicki to find out whether we needed to get to Chicago quickly for the waiting media, so I scanned the road a bit, thinking she might pull me off the river in urgency.

I never saw her, and Corps Lock No. Four was soon in view. Problem was, the view of Lock No. Four kept changing. As I got closer I realized that a barge, with its "three wide" nose was sticking out the end of the lock with the lock gates closed. I cautiously pulled in behind the lock into a small 100 x 1,000 foot pool.

The lockmaster was very nice to come down and tell me what was going on and that it would be a while before I could "lock through." He went on to explain this barge was the maximum allowed, five barges long by three barges wide with another barge "hipped" along side the tug for a total of 16 barges all pushed by one tug! These barges were carrying the capacity of 576 diesel trucks. When something that large is coming down the river, you want to get *way* out of the way.

It was so large, 950 feet long, that it had to push the front three lengths into the lock, then the back three, and then tie it all back together again. Wow! When it went by me out of the lock it seemed to go on forever.

I saw another barge coming down the river, so I went around the corner as soon as the tug cleared the end of the lock wall. The turbulence was tremendous out the back of the huge tug and threw me around quite a bit. The green light ushered me in, they dropped me down to the new river level, and I was gone in no time at all.

Now this next section of river was different. It was almost swampy with water flowing out of the main channel into other areas of water behind the trees. I passed up a few opportunities to slip out of the main channel and go exploring, but when I saw the barge that locked down behind me coming down, I took the next flow to the right behind the trees to escape its turbulence and multiple wakes.

Always before, the water would slip behind an island and merge back again almost immediately…big mistake! It was more like a swamp with low or no water movement, and it seemed to go further back and on forever.

To make things worse, my left pontoon was taking on water, something it had never done before. I moved back left every chance I could, but the main channel seemed to be gone. This went on for a long time, much longer than I was comfortable with.

Just when I thought I would have to pull Columbia up onto a grassy spot submerged in the river and try to lift it up enough to drain the water, a red buoy caught my eye a mile through an opening in the trees. I headed for it through water that seemed to be standing still. Just before I merged again into the main channel, I saw a sandy beach on the backside of an island whose front side was obviously on the main channel.

I headed for it and went to work hauling the waterlogged Columbia up on the beach and emptying out the left pontoon. Once done, I launched again and was back into the mainstream and alongside a village on the Wisconsin side.

Immediately after the town was Corps Lock No. Five and that's where all hell broke loose. When I got near the lock, it looked empty. As I approached the pull rope a barge was lifted up behind the gate... another "maximum allowed" barge. A guy yelled at me from its bow, "I'd move if I were you!" I looked at the nose of the barge, looked up river, and another barge had pulled off to the side waiting to go down. I looked over at the dam and the current pulling over the dam with the obvious crash and spray coming up from behind.

If I waited for both barges, I could be on the river after dark, and I knew they both had locking priority. I saw water going behind a little railroad bridge just 200 yards up river on the other side with the highway behind. I felt I had to go for it. I pushed hard into the current with all the "little engine" had. It was a stalemate. I was going nowhere. I pulled back over against the wall in front of the gate. The waiting barge was breathing down my neck like a wild bull ready to come out of the chute. The wall broke the current just enough, and I began to inch forward. I broke left around the end of the wall to the bank while I kept my eye on the pool of water under the bridge on the opposite bank.

I knew the current and Columbia were a stalemate before, so when I was even with the little railroad bridge I cut right and began to angle across the river with a 30-foot rooster tail spraying downstream off of Columbia's paddles. I had one barge below me and another ahead of me with the dam grabbing the rug out from under me as fast as it could, trying to pull me down and over its wall.

I fought for the right angle to get me to the distant bank as best I could, but the current was even stronger as I got out in the middle and the dam began to win.

It still looked like I could make the shore before the dam sucked me over, but I didn't know if the shore would offer enough protection to get me back up stream to the train bridge opening, freedom from the situation.

Just as I neared the shore and for the first time... the engine died! I didn't have time to try a restart; the dam was pulling me over fast. I got on the pedals immediately and pedaled with all I had in me. The dam seemed to pull harder and faster. I got to the shore just above the dam and grabbed onto the branches of a tree, hanging on for dear life itself. The current was so strong, even next to the shore, I couldn't get back upstream. Even after restarting and pushing the water logged "little engine" to its highest output, I could do nothing against the current. Then I had an idea. I traded full throttling the little engine with one hand and then the other as I grabbed limbs and pulled Columbia and myself upstream. Hand over hand, limb-by-limb I pulled Columbia along the shore until finally the bridge was mine.

I ducked right and under the railroad bridge to find the water led back to a swampy area grown up in trees. Dismantling Columbia into its three main parts of two pontoons and a bicycle, I hauled them up the railroad embankment. Once everything was up, I reassembled Columbia, started and throttled it to move along in the rocks and soft sand, while I pushed and walked alongside.

I was dripping with sweat by the time I reached the lock's service road. It was fenced with a security gate across the driveway. I pondered my options for quite a while. Then, just as I was ready to disassemble Columbia and lift all three parts over the fence, the gate mysteriously opened. I looked across the river; the lockmaster's tower was clearly in view of the gate. I waved a goodbye and thank you in the direction of the tower a quarter mile away and went quickly through.

Lock No. Five almost got me. I was thankful to have avoided the disaster. Seriously thankful that Columbia and I were still alive!

DAY 28 – Possibly My Most Dangerous Day

Everyday had its challenges and its rewards. Today's challenge was to get as close to Chicago in a day as I could. Columbia popped a tube the night before on the way to the motel in Winona. Vicki and I found a store open that had everything we needed, the motel provided a space, and by midnight the tire change was done. All this after the Lock No. Five experience!

This shook my confidence in making any miles at all today because I still had no back up wheel or gears. I was on the back up wheel now. We had not been able to get the original wheel fixed since we first entered Minnesota a week ago. I left instructions for Vicki to go ahead to Madison, Wisconsin, for a possible wheel job with Shawn to follow behind.

I completed the few miles I had along the river without incident, a wonderful drive overlooking my now beloved Mississippi. I crossed over the Mississippi on I-94 as it merged with U.S. Highway 61, and cheated Minnesota out of the last five miles of their interstate. I saw no other way across. I tried to make a go of interstate travel once again in Wisconsin. Once again I was caught at the first weigh station and escorted to one of the worst roads yet of my trip. I fumed to think the 8-foot wide paved shoulder with a rumble strip between me and traffic was taken from me, and I was made to run all day on a highway with a two-foot shoulder and no rumble strip because "the interstate was unsafe for vehicles under 40 miles per hour." All day trucks and cars screamed by two feet or less from my left shoulder, sometimes not even trying to reduce their speed below 70 miles per hour, a totally unnerving experience. At no time had I felt like my life was more in continual danger, more than on U.S. Highway 14 west of Madison, Wisconsin. Even after almost 3,000 miles of experience of highways, I was fighting to keep my nerve as each car and truck that passed was like a closer call with death.

Madison was even worse, with construction that forced me to residential streets with miles of stop-and-go traffic. By the end of the day I felt like someone who had spent all day literally dodging bullets. I had nothing but my bright clothing keeping me safe, all the while depending on the skill and concentration of the everyday, average motorist. Not a comforting thought. This was a day I just managed to survive, literally *not die*, and I knew it. God only knows how I made it with his protection. There were beautiful, picture perfect dairy farms all along the way, but I was made to concentrate on my mirror and a two-foot wide strip of rough shoulder all day long. The net result? Thirteen to fourteen hours of hard concentration and frequent pedaling for 180 miles. All things considered, it was an astounding amount of miles given the conditions. Vicki and I proved to be an unbeatable flat tire fixing team and a day of no flats was our reward. Totally unnerved and exhausted, I fell into bed. The fact that I'm even alive after this day is a miracle.

DAY 29 — On to Chicago!

Today I got up early and hit it again, determined to be in Chicago before the day was done. I continued the day I had left before, still on Highway 14. The conditions were the same; I was fresh now and had a 120-mile day ahead of me to finish this portion of the trek to Chicago. Of course, that would include 40 miles of city just getting into Chicago. I was equally determined to stop more frequently, pace myself, and snack along the way. I had two quick breakfasts at McDonald's as a result, an early one and a "brunch" one.

The farms were still beautiful, and the early Saturday morning traffic was as different as night and day, compared to Friday afternoon and evening traffic the day before. I felt more at ease, able to lift up my eyes and look around a bit. This went on for a couple of hours, until I came closer to wrecking Columbia than ever.

It was a long exit ramp, when the road widened to a four lane to cross an interstate. The height difference between the shoulder and the long, angled concrete ramp was about two inches. Just before the bike went out from under me, the knobby tire grabbed the edge of the concrete and swerved violently up onto the new surface. I wobbled and weaved out of control until it settled down into a smooth line again. My eyes fixed back on the two-foot wide strip of pavement, my relaxed country ride suddenly over. The traffic came alive as Saturday got into full swing, and it was more like the traffic of yesterday.   I was surprised when I whizzed past the Illinois state line. It just seemed to come up so quickly. I hate to say something like my next statement in this book, but I was so glad to be out of Wisconsin. I've had great times in Wisconsin before, but this was not one of them.

Highway 14 went from a two-foot shoulder immediately down to no shoulder in Illinois, and stayed that way for several miles, but traffic was light. It did redeem itself later on as I approached the outer limits of Chicago. As expected, it widened into a four lane and got busier. I was much more comfortable taking up the right lane knowing the other lane was there for the cars and trucks to pass, and the Saturday traffic was still light.

The Saturday feeling was light as well. The highway slowly turned into a 30-mile long four-lane street with shops and restaurants all along the way. An occasional "event" would have Saturday onlookers collected in crowds, and they would wave or thumbs up as I went by. First a motorcycle club, then an antique car club and then finally, a bicycle club! They waved and even began to try and catch me. I pedaled hard, to make a show that I was a bicycle. They pursued and when I last looked back had given up the chase, hands on hips, leaning on their bikes no doubt with a look of amazement on their faces. "How can that clumsy looking thing go so fast?" they might have asked, or maybe they heard the whir of "the little engine that could" and just thought it would be fun to try and keep up.

At any rate, Highway 14 couldn't have been a better route, and soon I was dumped right down onto the lakeshore and a beautiful park that went the length of the city, complete with a two-lane bicycle trail.

For the first time on my trip, at 2600 miles, I was riding in a world Pedal-Paddle was meant for, or so I thought. Again, it was Saturday afternoon and the trail was packed with bicyclists, in-line skaters, walkers, and joggers. I received a little resentment, as I took up so much space on the path. It was hard for me to get around people, and it was hard for them to get around me.

I admittedly came through the Windy City primarily for publicity. Vicki and our manager, Patrick, had met two New York girls with connections with both newspaper and TV. They had all insisted I take a couple of days in Chicago for publicity's sake. I needed to find a phone, a place to launch, and Vicki. My first priority would be a phone, but I soon ran face to face with big city attitudes and inconveniences. Folks were not all that helpful, and a phone was surprisingly hard to find. Before it was all over, I had to ride Pedal-Paddle half a mile down bumper-to-bumper traffic to find a phone card and a phone. I had wanted to keep my own cell phone with me, but both Vicki and Shawn had used it so much in the past week, Vicki had made me aware that several of these "connection" calls might be coming over my cell phone, so I felt I had to leave it with them.

With missed connections and the death of our beloved ex-president, Ronald Reagan, that same afternoon, TV was lost, at least for the day. We finally did hook up later, made repairs on Columbia and drove 20 miles out to a motel. My hard driving, 300 miles in two days ended without result. Our loss was extremely disappointing but compared to that of Nancy Reagan and the country...not such a big deal....

DAY 30 — A Little Good "News"

Vicki and Shawn and I started our week off at a little local church service near our hotel. It was very nice. The people were friendly, and their three-person church band was really good. It really soothed me a lot after my disappointing Saturday's introduction to the big city. Then we grabbed a great lunch at a famous downtown BBQ rib place. I was ready to get a few miles of Lake Michigan.

Just when all media seemed lost, Vicki got a call and said a newspaper writer and his young photographer were on their way, very excited about Pedal-Paddle Across America. So I tried to position myself for the interview. I did so by going four miles up the beach to launch. After three miles of Lake Shore Drive north, I had a rear flat tire that refused to air up again. Upon further inspection, I realized the tire and tube the bicycle shop professionals had put together for us had not been "slimed." I couldn't believe what was happening. Our second chance at media coverage in Chicago was being destroyed by a flat tire, one mile and five minutes from the interview.

What happened next, after the big city attitudes I had run into the day before, was amazing. A couple of Hispanic men, obviously with their boys, all on bicycles, came seemingly out of nowhere and started pulling out pumps and patches and all kinds of stuff.

I started to explain how difficult it was and all the tools necessary to change a flat on Columbia, but they were about to teach me a thing or three.

They pulled the tire off one side of the rim, pulled the tube out, pumped it up to find the leak, roughed it up, smeared glue on it, lit it with a match, put a patch on it, rubbed it down, reinserted it, pulled the tire back over the rim, aired it up and it was fixed! Without taking it apart! I tried to help, but I mostly just stood there with my jaw dropped in amazement!

Then it hit me. I'd been conned! I'd been in this "desperate for help" kind of situation before. Seemingly innocent, benevolent people come to your rescue, then stick their hand out for a ridiculous sum of money. I gritted my teeth as I asked, totally caught in my need and ready to pay the price. "How much do I owe you?"

"Oh, nothing! We just want to help! Will you show us how it goes in the water?"

I felt ashamed to be so accusing, pessimistic, and skeptical of their purely innocent gesture. I fell back in amazement. "Sure I will, follow me up the beach," and we all took off.

I was a little late so I pulled the engine trigger, rude to those who pedal in silence, and made my way up the beach bicycle path as quickly as the congestion would let me. I noted the distance and picked a suitable spot to launch.

A small crowd quickly gathered as we carried Columbia down the steps to the water, utilizing my newfound friends. I stepped into the water just far enough to lower the outside pontoon, then back on the beach to lower the other one. I caught glimpses of my new friends' faces enough to know they were in awe. Waving bye to the crowd, I pushed off from the shore to make my grand exit like the Wizard of Oz in his hot air balloon.

When I hit the throttle, a good 20-foot spray hit the beach and the kids all playfully went to yelling and screaming, but a voice from behind me was unlike all the others and not at all impressed.

"Sir! Sir! You can't launch that here," yelled a boy from a rowboat.

Usually nice to strangers, but totally frustrated by all but one of the days events, I snapped back, "Are you just now figuring that out? We've been launching it for quite a while!"

I immediately apologized, but he continued to threaten with the police throwing me in jail for sure, if I continued. I informed him that I was a law-abiding citizen and didn't have to be threatened to comply with their laws. I pulled up to shore and started to dismantle Columbia back to its original state. I was disappointed, again, in myself and frustrated to the boiling point.

The small crowd's reaction was mixed between "those jerks" and "wow, that was cool" so I was happy to have shown off Pedal-Paddle for the folks and gotten a little one up on the rotten system to boot. I suppose with a lot of people come a lot of rules, but I had been weeks in a world of "get in where you want, get out where you want" and this man-made park of a shoreline threw me for a loop. I apologized to the guys that had helped me for such a short show, but they were well pleased having just seen it go a few feet. I loped Columbia back down the path to meet the newspaper guy. No grand water entrance, just me and my machine.

When the *Chicago Sun Times* reporter arrived, he was great. He was very enthusiastic about Pedal-Paddle, the journey... the whole thing. His young photographer was his son, Josh, and, being a kid myself, it really helped me to smooth out the day's roller coaster ride to kid around with Josh.

I was so impressed with both Vicki and the reporter. She found a private boat ramp and marina just a half-mile away and talked our way onto it. The reporter was willing to come there to see Columbia in action, and he had to walk!

The reporter and his son had already asked a hundred questions and clicked a hundred pictures, but when I got to the dock's parking lot it started all over again and I was eating it up. Another small crowd pulled together as I put Columbia through figure eights in the parking lot while waiting my turn at the ramp.

Once on the ramp I gave them a show. I pulled away full throttle, pushing back a good 30-foot rooster tail of spray. They loved it! I stood on one side and then the other, pulling tight turns in the narrow passageway between boats. People were coming out of their yachts all over the harbor to watch and I was greatly encouraged, because I knew the excitement would translate into added interest in the news, and that's what we wanted.

A few more shots and it was time to put Columbia up while Vicki took the two of them back to their car. I answered a few more questions as the small crowd broke up. It was getting dark.

Vicki's little white rental car pulled up to the closed gate. Shawn jumped in, and as planned, I took off south on Chicago's fast and busy "Lake Shore Drive." With the little white car's flashing lights behind me, I held up traffic a bit at my 20 miles per hour top speed. Only in the city does that always get a few dirty looks, rude gestures, and angry shouts. But that's all okay. It's part of the big city life, I guess. This is Chicago, not Montana. People just don't have time to be slowed down here. And yet sometimes, just sometimes, when you least expect it, they'll stop and fix your flat.

DAY 31—The Windy City

We still had verbal promises to get TV news out on Monday if we would just stay in one place a couple of hours! Trying to blend media with actually getting somewhere for a change, I readied Columbia at 6:00 a.m. and launched about a mile from the motor home by 6:30.

There was no one around when I launched Pedal-Paddle at the ramp. I kissed Vicki goodbye as she traded me helmet for life jacket, then I pushed off.

As I slowly made my way out of the harbor into an easy breeze, one or two yachtsmen made their way to deck to wave at the curious craft and its captain. Although I was legal and had everything on board the coast guard required, I still was braced emotionally for another confrontation of "you can't do that here."

That confrontation never came from a single human being, but the wind itself was beginning to have more and more to say about my tiny craft being on Lake Michigan. As I passed by McCormick Place Civic Center, a huge, square, black building, fishermen poised along the land waved. Joggers and bicyclists stopped from time to time and just gawked at the sight of a bicycle bobbing up and down, spewing out a 30-foot spray as it pushed into the one-foot chop and two-foot rolls.

A high sea wall or large cement blocks the size of a pickup truck were the only shore line for the first mile, then two, then three. The wind got stronger, and the waves built in harmony with it. For the first hour or two, I was the only vessel as far as the eyes could see. Remarkable, I thought, considering I was on such a huge body of water and right in the middle of such congestion and masses on shore. I guess that's pretty typical of water almost anywhere, shores crowded with people, water empty. It was a Monday morning. I could see the streams of cars all taking their riders to work, as Lake Shore Drive flowed more and more heavily both north and south. Huge cranes and trucks were working along the shoreline as well.

After several miles, I saw what looked like a small beach and headed for it. Not knowing how long it might be before I was able to drain my pontoons or how bad it might get, I seized the opportunity. A small break in the wall of continuous big boulders was just large enough to create a small flat landing place on sand and pebbles. It was 9:30 a.m. and Vicki was to have reached all remaining news connections by 10:00, so I called to check on her progress. No answer, so I left a message and began to fill tanks.

I waited around for another 15 minutes or so, knowing I needed to get into the wind before it got worse. The lakeshore slowly curved around, and sooner or later I would be protected from the south wind, and, if I could hang in long enough, it would even be at my back on the Indiana side.

I could wait no longer and pushed off. The "little engine" fired, ran a few seconds and died. For the first time in the trip, it would not go. I wouldn't blame it if it never ran again, it had been through so much, but had done an admirable job until now.

Pedaling back to shore, I worked on it for 30 minutes or so, making sure it had fuel and such. I even let it give my finger a shock to make sure the magneto was giving fire to the spark plugs. I didn't have a spark plug socket so I was out of options. I called again and Vicki answered. I gave her a description of my location and instructions of all that might be needed, right down to the inconceivable thought of having to replace my little friend, even temporarily.

Shawn had to walk a good half-mile carrying the engine and parts over a walkway and onto the Lake Shore Park. The first thing we did was to remove the plug. It was fouled! We still didn't have a back up plug so I cleaned the one we had, replaced it, and sure enough, it fired right off.

I had been at this little isolated beach for two hours by now. I called Vicki, and she said reporters would be at the public beach two miles further down by 12:30. I had an hour and a half, so I asked her to meet me there with a hamburger and we'd have a picnic. It was her last day to be with me.

I pushed off once again and the "little engine that could" snapped to a whir at my command once again, creating its beautiful spray of water.

The wind seemed stronger, and swells were coming from around the point. I struggled around the point into view of the next stretch of shoreline…no beach. Columbia pushed on into the wind and waves across the shallow cove with great difficulty, bobbing up and down in the now three-foot waves hitting head on. The pontoons would not get all the water off from their tops before another wave would roll over them, keeping them completely submerged and fighting to break the surface.

The pontoons slowly filled with water, becoming heavier and heavier. I knew from miles of familiarity how to read their response. They were beginning to take on water through the bracket attachments on top. They had bounced and shaken for near 3,000 miles now and under these extreme conditions, it was showing.

As I came around the next point, the wind became even more violent. The waves washed over the pontoons so badly it must have looked like a bicycle alone was out there from the shore. Fact was, we were slowly sinking!

I fumbled in my pocket for my cell phone, as I worked and balanced Columbia in the waves. I called for Shawn to meet me on the boulder-strewn cliff walls of the shore — the only option I had. I fought to get in behind the point, and I pulled to the quietest spot I could find. Some of the boulders were just under water, a spot hardly the size of Columbia itself. Stepping off on to the boulders, I grabbed Pedal-Paddle and held it off the rocks as best as I could to keep it from breaking apart, banging on the boulders in the surf.

An older man came from up above, climbing on the upper boulders towards me. "Can I help?" he called with a strong accent.

"Please!" I shouted back. He held the left pontoon while I lifted Columbia off of it. Then, as he maneuvered it over to another boulder, I pulled Columbia up and onto the boulder I was standing on. As I pulled, I slipped and fell down between the boulders waist deep. I could have caught myself, but I held Pedal-Paddle up out of the water, trying to fill the job of the missing pontoon. I was able to keep Columbia up on the rock and climb back up on it myself. We then carefully tipped Columbia over, removed the right pontoon and slipped it around the back to shore and safety. Lifting each piece one boulder at a time, we finally got all three pieces up on top of the hill. In the process I poured five gallons, or 40 pounds, out of each pontoon, what I might expect after ten hours of riding, not one! This much water in the pontoons pushed Columbia to maximum capacity for a calm, still pond. To have kept it balanced and upright in the three-foot waves and wind gusts was nothing less than a miracle.

The man who came to my rescue was known by his friends as St. Joe, and I was right about the accent, he was from Czechoslovakia. Thanks, Joe! I couldn't have gotten out of Lake Michigan without ya!

Shawn showed up, we regrouped, put Columbia back together again and headed down the bicycle path, south to the next park. I waited another two hours on the promise of connections being made with the news, but the passing of our beloved president had changed all that more permanently than we had hoped.

I apologize, but I was anxious to get out of the Windy City. The big city was no place for an amphibious bicycle. I finally gave up, made plans to head south and east and took off through the streets of South Chicago. Much to my surprise, people of all races and even ages seemed to think Pedal-Paddle was cool. It thrilled me to get passing accolades from a group of teenage boys. The motorists in this section of town were actually the most courteous and sensitive to Columbia's unique needs on the road as I had seen in any town or city.

I passed through without incident. If Highway 14 on a Saturday morning was the way to come into Chicago, then Highway 12 on a Monday morning was the way to go out. I slipped through Gary, Indiana, and as the road curved around the lake northeast, I headed to Michigan City. I could actually feel the wind beginning to help instead of hurt my progress as I slowly curved around the bottom of Lake Michigan over about an hour's time.

The congestion, attitudes, and hassles of the big city fell slowly off of me as I cruised along, and Highway 12 helped. It was a very pleasant and wooded piece of smooth pavement as I passed by Indiana's Great Lakes Parks all along the shores on my left.

Let me stop for a moment and set the record straight on one subject. I had planned to sail across Lake Michigan but deferred to the shores and then finally, just got off the water altogether, for a couple of good reasons. It was not the $600 to $1,000 chase boat that got me. Nor was it my wife and Patrick's pleadings that changed my mind. It was what had become my infinite respect and appreciation for Columbia and "the little engine that could" that compelled me to pass up the trans-Lake Michigan trek. It had carried me 2600 miles to this point, and I wanted to see it, not me alone, finish the quest. It simply would not feel right to finish the run on the backup bike after all it had done. We could come back and fight Lake Michigan another day. To this date no one had ridden Columbia but me, and it was very personal to me to keep it as original and intact as possible and to finish this "Pedal-Paddle Across America" with the original of everything if possible.

Secondly, rivers double my speed, and banging into two to three foot waves and 30 mile per hour wind gusts cuts it to nothing; it's as simple as that. I felt it was foolish to sit around for possibly days to see if the Windy City was going to stop blowing, when I could get on to great rivers farther east.

I bypassed Michigan City and headed straight for South Bend where Vicki had a room ready and a restaurant picked out. It was our last night before she had to head back to Amarillo to work for a couple of weeks.

Day 32 — Ah! Indiana!

Indiana was a breath of fresh air from the minute I crossed the state line. The roads got better, smoother, and less crowded. The people seemed friendlier and more courteous on the road. The rivers, lakes, and farms were picturesque and well kept. It was just nice. I got up with a different attitude and looked at the map with a new understanding.

I no longer cared whether or not I got a piece of big cities or big water like Lake Erie. I was looking for any rivers that headed east at all. I found two in Ohio — the Maumee, beginning at Independence Dam, and the Portage, beginning at New Rochester.

I headed southeast on 33 to Highway 6 East. The drive was nice, and several stops for snacks and such made it even better. I had discussed a change in plans with Vicki, learning to go back and now report directly to Patrick my whereabouts on a one to two hour interval. It was a bit of a hassle but I believed it would pay off on publicity opportunities.

Okay, I'll go back and tell you about Vicki and myself having to go opposite directions for a while. I wasn't going to, because it was a private moment and I was a little embarrassed. Simple fact is, I cried. There, I said it. I don't often, but it was a combination of overwhelming emotion and sense of loss.

I needed her on this trip the whole way. She knows me like no one else. Things created by confusion that caused me great physical, mental, and emotional pain never would have happened had she been along — things too numerous to mention. She's my sounding board, my confidant, and my friend who understands. Things should have been in such an order, with the right people doing the right things that would have enabled her to be with me all along, but it just didn't happen in her department back in our company. So she had to be back in Amarillo, at least off and on, to see that our business kept heading in the overall right direction.

I did not want her to go. She should have been able to stay. This was the hardest thing I had ever done, and I needed her with me, but…I kissed her goodbye, not needing to say a word; my unintentional tears said it all. I simply got on the bike and rode, and let the miles, the scenery, and the beautiful day soothe my hurt and my loss. I had no choice but to finish what I had started. And so…I went on…determined to make the rest of the trip so fast I would see her in just a few days. That's the way I chose to say it…just a few days.

I was rolling along Highway 6 when two men in a car, one with a camera, flagged me down. So many people had wanted a picture of the crazy contraption I never thought much of it. When I stopped to answer their questions I discovered they were sponsored by several "Route 6" organizations and wrote articles for five newspapers and magazines. They were very interested in my trek and my machine and spent a good 30 minutes asking questions, taking notes, and snapping pictures. It was a really nice time and a really nice couple of guys.

We made our goodbyes, and I headed east again. I hadn't gone too far when I noticed the familiar wobble of a flat back tire. I was so mad at myself for not picking up a can of "Fix a Flat" nor a pump. I pushed the bike across the highway into a driveway under a tree and pondered what to do.

There were two houses in the whole mile and next to each other. I noticed the house next door had several riding lawn mowers out front and a "for sale" sign on one of them.

I walked over but couldn't find anyone. Sitting there by the garage was an air compressor on wheels. I looked around and an electrical outlet was standing up in the flowerbed. It was hard to believe, but here was an opportunity to move on.

I looked around again, rolled the compressor over to the outlet and plugged it in. With no switch and no gauge it came immediately to life, pumping precious air into its tank. "God is good!" I thought.

A man in a van pulled into the driveway and I got ready to apologize for my intrusion, but he just wanted to look at the riding mowers. I explained my situation. He laughed and said he'd come back later.

I rolled the tank next door, filled my tire, rode the bike over to the riding mower's garage to give the Slime a chance to find the hole, and went back for the tank. As I walked along I pondered why he might work out in front of his house on the highway, but it was obvious he could watch things, for one, and also I had been honked at by passing friends at least five times in 30 minutes; not a bad deal!

I wrapped a dollar around the air hose as I put the tank back where I found it, chuckling as I did so, imagining his bewilderment upon his discovery of the dollar. But, it made me feel a little better about the theft. The Slime held and I rolled on.

The Ohio state line came not long after. Three states to go! The rest of the day was uneventful. I was to meet our Michigan Pedal-Paddle representative in Defiance, Ohio, for dinner. With the two 30-minute interruptions, I rolled into town only 15 minutes late, found him, and had a great dinner. We'd never met before, and he was a delight, an exceptionally knowledgeable man, who had obviously studied his subject well. We discussed forthcoming improvements to the product, all a result of my nearly 3,000 miles, and it was good to visit with a man more my own age for a while.

He headed back north to Michigan, and Shawn and I went on to find a place for the R.V. Another 180 miles was done. It had been really good to get moving again, and to find new rivers to go down along the way.

DAY 33—I Want My Maumee!

I went to bed and woke up with one thing in mind. Back on a river! I've fallen in love with Pedal-Paddling rivers. I think the ultimate calling for Pedal-Paddle, as a product, is to paddle down a river, fold it up, pedal up the river, and then paddle down again, over and over.

I love the scenery, the winds are usually better, and I was down in the river canyon and more protected. I love how it doubled my speed, or in my case, the distance.

The Maumee River in Ohio was perfect, just deep enough, wide enough, and long enough between dams to add 50 miles to my water total. It was a southwest to northeast run, but still it headed in the general direction.

I went the first hour without seeing anyone. Then one man on the bank yelled for me to look so he could get me to wave for a picture. An hour or two later a single small pontoon boat steamed up river past me, all aboard waving at the strange contraption. I waved back because Columbia was too busy.

After a while longer a little town began to roll by on the banks, and then a bridge came into view for added excitement. It was a great day. I felt at peace and unthreatened by my surroundings for the first time in a long time.

With the town came boats and jet skis. All were spying the strange visitor to their waters, and most waved or "thumbs upped" their appreciation.

I had gotten really good at making sign language, showing that the pontoons folded up and the craft also went on land. This usually got even more appreciation. This day I was also able to sign I had been 3,000 miles, 500 on water. Again, more signs came back of "wow" in some form.

My signing was twofold. It answered their obvious, unspoken questions, and it let them know I needed to keep going without actually having to say so. It saved me from having to stop almost continually or be rude and just keep going. At any rate, I had created a system that seemed to work for the curious, which was just about everyone, and for me.

Bridges were another thing I had grown to love about rivers. There were footbridges, road bridges and railroad bridges of all kinds and types. Bridge architecture in itself is fascinating. But, here's a thought. I've never been on a road that didn't tell you with a sign what river you're going over, but I've never been on a river that told you what highway the bridge was on. Why doesn't somebody do that?

Anyway, it was a great day, with lots of ducks and geese and birds, and fish that jump straight up out of the water, and trees and houses and towns, and one beautiful county courthouse, and all that stuff…. Then it rained.

I didn't mind the rain. I had a poncho to pull over me, and it was warm. I really kind of enjoyed it. But then it got late and colder. It back-winded Columbia's spray on me, and I got cold, and then I got miserable.

I just had on a bathing suit, a life jacket and a plastic poncho. This was okay for the first six hours, but it just got too late and too long.

I went from "I want my Maumee" to "I want my mommy" pretty quick. My teeth began to chatter, and I felt really stupid for not being better prepared for the day to turn colder or longer than expected.

I would stop from time to time to ask "How long till Mary Jane State Park?" It seemed everyone knew it was just around the next bend in the river, only it never was. I finally bailed out and phoned Shawn instructions on how to find me. I ended up just a mile or so from the ramp where he was waiting for me, but I didn't care. I justified "I would have been dead by then" and was glad to be off of the river.

We bedded down at the state park, and I was warm and dry. Like so many other things in life, my cold, wet, misery faded away, and all I had left were the memories of a beautiful day on the Maumee.

DAY 34 – Plying the Portage River

I started my day by making up the two miles back up the road where I had come out of the river. Then just three miles south and I was back on U.S. Highway 6 headed east. It was raining from the minute I left the park, but the same poncho that covered only a bathing suit the day before now covered my bright orange bib overalls and parka. I was wet on the arms and legs, but comfortable.

The trucks passing by covered me in a mist, but everyone was courteous on the road. I only had an hour and a half to two hours of these conditions before I was at another northeast bound river, the Portage, where I was going to get off and ask the locals if anybody ever canoed it.

Just as I crossed the first of two forks of the Portage, a tractor sales and service shop was within a few yards of the bridge. I pulled into their yard and up to the shop door. As usual I couldn't ask any questions until I had answered a few. When it was my turn, I inquired about the river and found "it is canoed on rare occasions when the water is up." It had been raining all night and the day before, so I headed for the river. I pulled Columbia down the embankment and lifted it over a pile of large rocks to the river, one at a time. First the back, then the front, until I had it in the water about eight inches deep. I lowered the left side into the water then the right, gently onto the rocks. I tied on two gas tanks, all the while sizing up the river.

Pedal-Paddle would barely float the 50-foot wide creek. Rocks stuck up everywhere but sparsely enough to get through. I was taking a chance on the tractor mechanic's word and the fact that the two tributaries came together just a half-mile down from the bridge.

I pushed off gently and hit the engine. I had been tying off the throttle almost immediately in the other rivers, but here I kept a finger on the throttle trigger and a constant gaze on the small river for obstacles.

Along with rocks, several tires were discarded in the river, the first I'd seen on my journey. The fork provided a little larger river as promised, but just a little. It added only a few inches of depth and a few feet of width to the river.

I felt safe on the river, but I was concerned for Columbia's pontoon bottoms, scratching and scraping on the rocks. I was not afraid so much for the pontoons as for the large Pedal-Paddle decals that, when raised, provided two billboards advertising the vehicle.

It was a gorgeous little ride, lined with huge trees and occasional house developments, but I did drag the bottom more than all other rivers combined. At times the whole river squeezed itself over a shelf of rock and I got off and walked Columbia over. In fact, it became a routine every 100 yards to a quarter mile or so. A shallow but passable pool, then a thin rapid over rocks, then back to a shallow pool again. In these sometimes long pools, I saw all kinds of birds and more fish than I can ever remember. Some of the fish were so large, the whole pool rippled when they moved. They created more of a surface disturbance than Columbia... now that's a big fish!

I looked at one rock because it looked like a snake had raised its head up to look at me. As I got closer I could see the submerged shape of a turtle shell almost one foot in diameter. His neck must have pushed his head six to eight inches out of the water; I'd never seen anything like that before. I had no idea a turtle's neck could be so long.

Another treat of the day was a kind of bird I'd never seen before. They scooted across the water in packs of five to ten. They looked kind of like the bugs that swarm on the water, but these were kind of a brownish, small bird.

The best show of all came when I herded a family of geese along the shore. It was cows in Montana and now geese in Ohio. They stayed just ahead of me, the mom and dad coaxing the three little ones along. As I began to overtake them, the daddy broke away forward, splashing and squawking and acting like he was wounded and couldn't fly. When I got right even with the mom and three chicks, she corralled them in behind a protruding low branch in a second of time and joined the daddy in their show. Doing all they could to draw my attention, they kept up the act the entire length of the pool, each taking their turn. Then at the end of the pool they took flight, circled back over me and went to find their little ones again. An altogether fascinating experience, it was really neat to see, first hand, how they decoyed to protect their young.

The only time I knew the world was still alive was when going under bridges. I was only hailed by two fishermen on the banks in two different locations along the river and one little girl, who ran along her riverside backyard fence to keep up with me as I waved to her.

With a light sprinkling of rain off and on all day, this was a day of nature and concentrating on getting Columbia down this creek-sized river. It was another great river day.

Shawn was waiting for me on a footbridge just a couple hundred yards before the county bridge with video in hand, video I'm sure I'll enjoy for years, to help spawn the memories of this day. And, like you, I'll have this little book to retell the tale of my trip, my rare trip down a river the locals seldom even try to navigate and few will ever see.

The three-inch draft of Pedal-Paddle once again went where even canoes and kayaks would have had trouble going and took me through nature and beauty rarely seen. *Thanks again, Columbia, and good night....*

DAY 35 — After Rain There is…Rain!

After two days of rain I got up to the sound of more rain. I got partially dressed to go out and get started when it got harder and pounded the roof pretty good. I was beat anyway, so I just fell back in bed and pulled the covers over me, half asleep and half listening to the rain.

I got up and wrote day 34 and waited again. It seemed to slow a bit, so I got a trash bag and headed out the door. Shawn and I assembled Pedal-Paddle, and he helped me slice the trash bag into two equal squares. Then we duct taped the plastic around my legs.

Before, as my legs got soaked, the water would saturate the bib overalls and then slowly fill my boots with water, I guess I should have bought the more expensive "water proof" bibs instead of the "water resistant" ones.

I pulled over the plastic poncho, now half shredded from the wind, and took off. The rain got worse, then better, and then worse, and then better. Even at 22 miles per hour it stung my face at times, but I didn't mind. This was wet, but compared to the freezing rain of Montana and North Dakota, this was a walk in the park.

Oak Harbor was the closest I would come to Lake Eerie. Just like Lake Michigan, I let the weather decide whether or not we would do a little, a lot, or any at all of the big water. A blowing rain out of the northeast answered that question. Again, there were more easterly flowing rivers in eastern Pennsylvania to be had; to put up with big water's big waves simply wasn't worth it.

I headed south for U.S. 20. It was under construction but close to completion, so I rode protected behind orange barrels for miles.

When it did turn back to normal, it was a great road and had a good shoulder. I stopped in Clyde, Ohio, for a burger and spent 30 minutes talking with a very excited 71-year-old that wanted to write me a check for a couple of Pedal-Paddles on the spot. I deferred him to the office but really enjoyed his enthusiasm for the contraption as well as the trip.

Highway 20 became a two lane. I blew a back tube and called for back up. I could've changed it myself, but I wanted to get the original wheel and bearings back on the bike. Some really nice folks let me use their carport should the rain, which took a vacation, go back to work again.

By the time Shawn arrived at the scene I had the bike strung up and disassembled. We quickly replaced the original back wheel and I was on my way. Just seven miles later as 20 headed directly towards Columbus, I angled off on 303 to shoot straight across the state and split between Columbus and Akron. After Chicago, I wanted to be sure and avoid big cities all together, until I make the unavoidable New York City area.

Not another seven miles had gone by before the original wheel with new tube and tire was flat. My day on the road was ended. It was okay, though. An old friend,

Michael, and his wife, Katie, had recently moved to Ohio. They met us for dinner and we had a great time talking of old times and the new trip. Sixty miles for the day was disappointing but all things considered... not bad.

DAY 36—Pennsylvania, Here We Come!

I started the day with breakfast at the same restaurant where we had dinner the night before. It seemed like the right thing to do since we had spent the night in their parking lot. Afterward I had Shawn drive out to the spot where I had the flat. I saw no reason to re-pedal these 30 minutes.

Highway 303 just east of Wakeman is so sparsely traveled we stopped right in the middle (on our side) of the highway; it was so hard to get on and off anyway. We had Columbia unloaded and gone in less than three minutes.

Highway 303 was the perfect choice. It was less traveled and splits right between Akron and Cleveland. As I drove through Brunswick, Ohio, I declined to let the Brunswick High School cheerleaders wash my Pedal-Paddle as I drove through town. They were hard to turn down and Columbia needed a bath badly, but we had miles to go and I did not need a drowned engine. 303 goes right through the middle of Cuyahoga Valley National Park, a beautiful drive but so hilly my legs were burning. It goes through Peninsula, a neat little town with woodsy shops and antiques.

This would be a great place for Vicki to spend a day; she absolutely eats this kind of thing up, and could shop for hours... I'd just as soon look at the hills, trees and streams, so I did.

After this area the road flattened out a bit. I love watching the farms roll by at 20 miles per hour. You just see more, and sitting high on the bicycle seat helps too.

Before 303 had a chance to dead end into Warren, we took Highway 534 north to 305 east to go around. An Ohio State Trooper pulled me over just to see "what in the heck I was doin'." Just about everybody I see has that look on their faces, but he had the lights and badge to stop me and ask. I pulled into a driveway. He stopped in the right lane, blocking traffic while we talked, and his parting words were, "Try not to block traffic".... Go figure.

I hit Highway 5 headed northeast back to Highway 6, and it just got greener and hillier and more wooded. Before I knew it, I passed the "Welcome to Pennsylvania" sign. Something inside leapt as I passed into my next to last state.

At Jamestown I continued northeast on 322 and when I hit U.S. 6 at Conneaut Lake, I was in "motorcycle city." They were coming from everywhere, roaring as they went.

It was Saturday evening and I could have ridden a couple more hours, but I had already seen signs of partying and alcohol, and something inside told me to get off the highway; I had done enough.

Shawn and I had both seen signs for Conneaut Lake Park so we loaded up Columbia and headed for it. The joke was on us, as it turned out to be an amusement park, but across the street was a RV park with all the hookups. We pulled in, they had a spot, and it was "home sweet home" for the night.

I fell asleep listening to a father play with his children late into the night. They were on vacation. I loved that sound....

DAY 37—Oh, My God! I'm in Heaven!

Shawn and I started out pretty early. I cooked a bacon and egg breakfast and Shawn drove us back to the vegetable and fruit market where we had loaded Columbia up. It was Sunday so I headed east on Highway 6 while looking for a church we might like to visit. Just two or three miles down the road, there it was. I went in and listened to them practice the morning's songs for a few minutes. It was about 9:00 a.m., and they told me of the "continental" breakfast at 9:30 and that the service started somewhere around 9:45. Perfect!

Shawn saw Columbia on the side of the highway and pulled in. I climbed in and got more appropriately dressed. We entered to meet the nicest people, have great morning snacks, be a part of good music and get inspired to meet the challenges of the week ahead.

Afterwards we made our good-byes but not until we gave in to their insistence to pray for our safety. Much appreciated!

The day was to be short and end us up in the Allegheny National Forest and a campground on Ministers Creek. Again motorcycles were everywhere and for good reason. There were little two lane blacktop roads running everywhere, through gorgeous woods, with rivers and streams all along the way.

To recap our path, and it's not easy, we were to take 6 east to State 27, to State 227 East, to State 127 South, to U.S. 62 North, to State 666 East, all in 50 to 60 miles. It was worth it.

I had to pull several hills, every one sending my legs to the burning point. On one hill, I found that one fuel tank was mysteriously empty with two untouched. So I stopped to clip it off in a driveway. Something red on the side of the driveway caught my eye, and I found myself picking wild strawberries and popping them in my mouth. That was a first for this "dry lander."

Away again, I stopped for pictures with some locals, and once for fuel, especially since the tanks were behaving so strangely.

As I crossed over the Allegheny River I was taken aback at its size. This far up in the hills, it still flowed at least 100 yards wide. I sure wished it headed east, but it doesn't. It did, however spawn new hope that some of the "creeks" on the eastern slope might be big enough to float.

I chugged slowly up Highway 666 mostly following along the upstream direction of Tionesta Creek. This "creek" is still a good 50 yards wide and I passed many canoes along the way. I felt Columbia jump towards the creek several times, but I held the reins tight and made her stay on land. We both wanted to hit the water bad but we just couldn't go west, maybe some other time....

I stopped for a sandwich and made sure I was headed the right direction. These smaller roads are a little tricky. Also, I was taking at least an hour longer than I thought I would.

I was headed right. The hills were just slowing me down and I was going generally up. I hadn't seen Shawn all day, and he was supposed to "stay close," so I was bothered by that as well. I wondered if he had listened to my update messages and decided to take a longer, less hilly route and somehow gotten ahead of me. When I arrived at Ministers Creek campground there was no Shawn, RV, or trailer.

I pulled into the campground and said out loud, "Oh, my God! I'm in heaven." If I had painted a picture in my mind of the perfect camping spot, it would be this. Our campsite had a long entry for the 55' rig Shawn was driving. It totally blocked us from the little trail that led back to three more sites and a tent camping area. A campfire pit, with wood left, and a picnic table were there, both just a few inches from the picture perfect creek. The creek and campsite were thick with the Allegheny's landmark giant oaks and pine trees. The creek gurgles 30 to 40 feet wide and butterflies accent the paradise with movement and color.

I put my helmet on the table, and my gloves on the firewood to say "mine." I parked Columbia just off the road and prayed that Shawn would be along before I was forced, by approaching nightfall, to have to leave to find a room in the next town.

I hiked up the creek a bit and hadn't been gone 20 minutes before I recognized the faint rumble of our rig pulling in. By the time I got back down, Shawn had already followed the trail of my strewn breadcrumbs and was parked in exactly the spot I had pictured.

I didn't have to say a word. The look on his face said it all. The folks back at the office had been begging us to slow down. We were poised to finish our 8-week trip in just six weeks. Within seconds we agreed to take a day off in paradise. My second day off in the trip and my first *real* day off. No malls, sight seeing, or lock inspecting.

We built a fire and used it to cook a great dinner of steak, corn still in the shucks, baked beans, and toast. We ate like animals with no one to apologize to.

As night fell, our cooking fire became a campfire. The smell of the oak wood was a rare treat. The setting became nothing less than magical as the fire began to light up the underneath side of the branches looming over us, and stars shining in the few holes the tree canopy provided. Fireflies twinkled, first here, then there, as though Tinkerbell showed up with all her cousins by the dozens. Distant lightning would add a faint splash of light overhead from time to time. I was so tired and beat, but it was really late when I finally dragged myself away from the fire. It was next to impossible to leave. *What I've just written is the only thing constructive I'm doing today. See you back on the road tomorrow and we'll see if we can find some more water to float down!*

DAYS 38 & 39—My First *Real* Day Off!

If the evening at Minister Creek Campground was magical, the morning was mystical. As I stepped out to cook breakfast by campfire there was a fog on the creek that rose faintly up into the trees. I prepared a fire and cooked breakfast in unbelievable silence. Only natural sounds were heard until they were finally broken by the sound of a distant service truck on the road. I heard it stop, pick up trash, and move on. That was it.

Just as I promised myself, I did nothing all day but a little reading and a short hike. I never take naps, but never say never. Shawn told me I was out for two hours. I was amazed. I had slept very well the night before. I guess I just needed the rest.

The evening was a repeat of the last but earlier and with hot dogs. We thought it was over really early as the sky became black and a thunder shower sent us running for the RV. But it cleared quickly. Nothing more than a brief show of power. If it didn't rain, it wouldn't be so green and beautiful.

We coaxed the fire back to life but still got to bed relatively early. The repeat of last night's star and Tinkerbell show was still just as dazzling, but I was getting psyched up to get some miles in tomorrow.

Day 39 started with a quick breakfast cooked inside. I backed the rig out of its spot all the way to and across the highway, the only way to get it out. We checked the bicycle's pouch to see if all I needed was there and I took off.

If you're aware of the Biblical reference to the number 666, the highway is an enigma as it took me through heaven on earth. The hardwood forest is boring, that is if you get tired of beauty, and more beauty. The road was narrow but I don't think three cars passed me in the hour back to U.S. Highway 6 at Sheffield, Penn.

The route continued east through more of the same natural surroundings but added more people, more cars and trucks, neat little towns every few miles and a nice road with a wide shoulder to take you safely through it all, or as safe as highway travel at 20 miles per hour gets.

Shawn and I played leap frog for 40 miles or so, so he was only 10 miles behind me when I ruined a tube and a tire coming into Port Allegany (that is the correct spelling as opposed to the Allegheny River. Why, I don't know).

Anyway, it conveniently blew right beside the city park. I took Columbia apart, placing the pontoons by the road and the bike under a tree to work on it, while two older gentlemen looked on in silence. I asked where I might find a phone to get Shawn to bring a tire. They pointed down the street a block to a service station and said they'd watch my stuff.

I went, called, and came back with an ice cream for all three of us. I sat and ate and talked for a while and then I went to work. I had it all torn down by the time Shawn arrived and we replaced the tire and tube on the rim. It was then I noticed several spokes were broken near the hub in this original wheel assembly. We changed the tire and tube over to the backup.

I had already made the decision to replace the drive chain on the engine side. I so wanted every part of the original bike to make the trip if at all possible, but just knew I would be on the water when it broke and all I would hear is a plop and it would be gone forever. I had plans for this chain. It had served in training and 3600 miles of the trip. I figured it had about 4,000 miles on it, and though it may seem silly, I cherished that old chain. Think about it, it had driven the whole apparatus 4,000 miles without failure and had stretched a total of four inches in the doing. Now, that's tough!

I put the chain up for safekeeping and put on the new chain. With all done I took off again, two hours of my day spent in repairs.

I hadn't gone 10 miles when the tube went flat again. I checked it to find four holes. I spent another hour, dismantling Columbia's rear wheel assembly again. I washed the rim and tire off in a large puddle left by the rain. I went over the tire and rim again and again and could find no reason at all for the holes. I finally decided to just put it all back together with a new tube from my carrying bag. I took off down the road again, but it was getting late.

I had a great day in beautiful country but two flats had cut me to just 80 miles or so. I limped into Coudersport, ate and wrote this daily report. Shawn and I spent the night in the restaurant parking lot, here by the highway.

I'm determined to get up early and find some water tomorrow; the water I should have found today. But, that's life on a motorized, amphibious bicycle. It's a one of a kind.

There's no manual for what we're doing. You just go, and take what you get, and deal with it as best as you can. I'll forget the flats and remember the beautiful trees, streams, hills and towns. That's all of our job in life. Hang on to the good stuff. The good memories.... Good night.

DAY 40—Still in Search of Water!

I didn't sleep well at all. The little highway seemed to stay busy all night. My decision to sleep on the backside of the restaurant parking lot was a bad one. Finally at 6:00 a.m., I had all I could take. With just enough light, I wasted a little time doing odds and ends, then prepared Columbia and took off. The early morning was foggy but safe enough, as everyone on the road seemed to be moving slow.

We don't get much fog in Amarillo so I really kind of enjoyed the eerie way it made everything look. Just outside of town it got even thicker, to the point it started to seem dangerous. There was hardly any shoulder on the road, but just as I thought of pulling over for a while, a shoulder appeared and invited me to keep going.

I was a little cold, but a couple of steep hills took care of that. At the top of the third hill a sign said "Allegheny Summit 2424 feet." That meant it would be mostly downhill from here.

I saw a canoe rental place and got excited thinking water deep enough to float on might be going my way. But west-running water had only made it to south. Not quite east yet.

I went on a couple of hours and hadn't seen Shawn all morning, so I ducked in for a quick bite in Troy. The map said Sugar Creek had fully formed and ran east from here. Some call it luck, I call it blessing, but in the fast food restaurant was a man studying a detail map of Pennsylvania just like the one I had for Montana.

A quick inquiry and I was talking to the man whose job it was to study all the streams and rivers of eastern Pennsylvania for insect control! Another man about my same age, Herb, whose hobby was canoeing, also entered the conversation.

They schooled me on Sugar Creek; its depth and flow not suitable for travel this time of year, as well as every other river. Where to get in, where to get out, what to expect...you name it. I was then invited to dinner at the house of the canoe enthusiast on the river; a right perfect stop for the end of tomorrow on the Susquehanna River.

The Susquehanna was floatable, it did go southeast and it was just 20 miles ahead. With detailed instructions on where to get in, exactly how much I could do in the remainder of the day, and where I could get out to spend the night, with instructions for Shawn how to get the RV down on the river; I was off again with hearty "Thank you's" all around, especially up above.

I followed the instructions to a little park and boat ramp looking right up at US Highway 6 in Towanda. After waiting a while for Shawn I called to find out he was just over the bridge with a flat tire of his own. His quick thinking, however, had a life jacket and my extra gasoline on their way by way of a nice lady that had stopped and sweetly but naively asked, "Can I help?" He put her right to work, and within minutes of my inquiry I had gas and life jacket in hand. A few minutes more and I was launched onto the beautiful Susquehanna. It was 4 p.m. and my guide had calculated a 4-hour ride for me to reach the take out point approximately 20 to 24 miles down, "depending on how many 'shortcuts' you take."

I immediately hit 2-foot rapids and the race was on! What a ride. An amusement park and nature ride all in one. I love rivers. They're kind of a log ride/roller coaster ride all in one, and if you're really bad at keeping your craft headed down stream you can throw in the tilt-a-whirl as well!

Like a good roller coaster the river gave thrills then long, still pools, then more thrills then a long, still pool. It's great to try and pick out where you think the ride's the fastest and then ride it out to see how you did.

Being my first time on the river I picked out some winners, and I picked out some losers, but I never banged a rock or dragged bottom once, an overall win.

Another thing my guides had told me of were bald eagles. I was not disappointed. I saw at least a half dozen on the trip, soaring high above the wooded and rocky hills. How majestic. Other birds like cranes were along the way as well, giving the long pools a chance to show off what they had to offer me.

There were a few people and a couple of boats on this 20-mile stretch, but given its proximity to major cities, I was shocked at its seclusion.

You're not going to believe the next part of my story, but at exactly one minute until 8 p.m. I looked up and saw the motor home and trailer. How's that for guesswork? I wouldn't be at all surprised if it was straight up eight o'clock when I pulled Columbia ashore.

We had found water once again, and it was great! It's just safer and I feel more free on the water. I can enjoy the beauty instead of concentrating on staying on the edge of the road, flat tires, and not getting run over by cars and trucks. The Susquehanna River was especially nice as it came as a totally unplanned surprise.

DAY 41—A Day on the Susquehanna

This morning, like all the night before, was overcast and rainy. I only had nine hours to the take out point so I was in no hurry.

This was not a 7:00 a.m. get out and get it day. My river guide, Herb, had been so exact the day before on distance and time, I was very confident today would be very close on the numbers.

It stopped raining about 8:30 so I was on the river by 9:00. It was clearing so nicely I wore simply a bathing suit, t-shirt and dive booties and, of course, my life jacket.

The river was just as I had left it — gorgeous. There's really not much to tell. The river ran fast and slow intermittently as before, fish jumped and darted out of my way, birds of all types flew and the shore, like the river itself, was intermittently low with houses and campers on one side, high with steep hills and forest on the other.

As for the birds, there were egrets, eagles, blue heron, cranes and probably a hundred others I can't name, a veritable bird watcher's paradise.

The fish were fairly common as well, until that one. I thought it was a river submarine. I had seen big fish move the water all day. I really didn't see the fish, just the water move. You know, a wave created by something big underwater that makes a wake like a boat. In fact, these fish wakes were so big they made a bigger wake than my Pedal-Paddle. Well, this one I saw, must have been five feet long and built like a torpedo. I was excited that one finally let me get close enough to see what it was. From Columbia's high vantage point, it was picture perfect down in the water. Man! It was big!

Another interest of the day were these little bugs on top of the water. They were little black bugs, about the size of a pinhead, but, boy, could they move. They would get out in front of Columbia and actually keep up at four to five miles per hour, darting back and forth. I imagined that's what a bunch of jet skis must look like from an airplane. But when I got so close I was just about to run over them, they would submerge and dart left or right almost as fast underwater as on top. They provided great entertainment throughout the day.

The only variation to my day was the one manufacturing plant on the shores and the coming and going of rain. The rain was really kind of pleasant, even in a bathing suit. I just tightened my life jacket down for insulation and warmth and I was fine. Just as I got out, it began to get heavier. A few thunder rumbles made me glad to see the public boat ramp of Tunkhannock.

Herb had lived on the river since age five and had invited Shawn and me for dinner at his cottage on the river! I arrived at the ramp at about 5:30 p.m., again within minutes of when Herb said I would.

There was no RV, trailer, or Shawn to meet me, so I asked a couple that were fishing if I was in the right place. They assured me I was, so I pulled Columbia up on the shore of large round smooth stones and ran up the dock and road to find shelter. It was raining hard.

I was climbing the ladder to a caboose turned playhouse when I heard a horn honk behind me. I turned to see Herb in his vehicle waving me in out of the rain.

Once inside his SUV, I learned Shawn was pinned down in Scranton with tire problems and Herb was the cavalry. He had a raincoat for me and followed me to where the trailer was parked in a Wal-Mart parking lot.

He went on to fix dinner with his wife, Jane, and I went into Wal-Mart for a rain suit and Gatorade.

Shawn was there before too long, and we loaded Columbia into the trailer and me into the motor home. I shaved and dressed while Shawn drove, and before 10 minutes had expired we were pulling into Herb and Jane's driveway.

Their place was perfect as far as I could see. A log cabin type home in a veritable botanical garden. Hors d'oeuvres, steaks from the grill, and veggies from the garden and I knew I had died and gone to heaven. Conversation was refreshing as well with Jane's interest in music; my degree is in music from West Texas A&M University in Canyon, Texas. Herb's knowledge of the river was amazing. He talked about its birds and fish, and showed us his wall of prize plaques from canoe races on the river. It was from our conversations that I named several of the bird species I had seen earlier. He went on to educate me of the river's unique currents, the little bugs that fascinated me so called skeeters, and the huge fish known by the locals as muskies.

Just when I thought the evening couldn't get any better, they brought out ice cream topped with Herb's homemade maple syrup. I hated to leave this gracious and hospitable couple, but it was time to go.

A quick drive back to the parking lot, and it was easy to fall asleep. *What a great day, and I found a couple of people along the way as beautiful as the surroundings. Thank you, Herb and Jane.*

DAY 42—Trouble in Bunches Like Bananas!

Day 42 started with a knock on the RV door. I was actually awake, up and writing "Day 41" since I crashed asleep the night before. We were to have an easy morning on the river followed by an afternoon on land headed for the start of the scenic Delaware River.

The knock came from the knuckles of a local reporter. He apologized for the intrusion but explained it was his only opportunity to get a story before he flew off to L.A. I was not in the least upset and bounced out the door to show off my contraption. I was just about to leave for the river and a water demonstration, when Herb showed up with jars of his homemade maple syrup and Jane's homemade relish. I "relished" the thought of seeing him and the jars. (Bad joke).

It was kind of funny he showed up when he did, because I was just telling the reporter of the couple's amazing hospitality. They both followed me down to the water, and I launched Columbia for a show off session! The reporter was really nice and seemed very impressed and enthusiastic about Pedal-Paddle.

He had to rush off, so I thanked him for coming. Herb and I were left to say goodbye again, but not until we talked way too long about the river and related things. I had to go so we vowed to stay in touch. I pulled the start cord, hopped on and waved goodbye.

It was a very pleasant three hour run down to Falls Landing, but when I arrived I was disappointed to find all the reporters that were interested the evening before had scrambled to a weather disaster scene 50 miles below us. That's the way it goes in the news business. A blown down barn and trees take precedence over the final days of setting seven world records. Can you tell I was a little upset? Is anybody besides me sick and tired of disaster, chaos, rape, murder and pillage news? Maybe people would do fewer bad things if they weren't so well covered on TV. Enough. I'll move on to *my* next disaster.

I got out of the river and the pedal gears wouldn't hold. They just slipped, and the pedals freewheeled. Shawn and I WD-40'd the cassette until it would intermittently work. So I took off.

I hadn't gone a mile before I realized the gear shifter had rusted to the point it wouldn't shift. Shawn stopped, and together we took apart the shifter cable system and WD-40'd all its components as well. It was back as good as new, so Shawn took off ahead of me to get the spare wheel in Scranton he had left the day before.

I got about five more miles and the drive chain on the motor broke where we had to add two offset links, my fault. I got that fixed and within a mile the back tube blew. I think it was about our twentieth blow out! Now remember, we didn't have a flat the first 500 miles!

The silver lining to all this string of misfortune came in the form of a silver-haired lady soon to be 94 years old. She let me use her phone, and we sat side by side in her beautiful front yard while I waited for Shawn and she waited for her daughter to pick her up.

Shawn, on the other hand, was dealing with two freak flats of his own on new tires! My new friend's daughter had a miscommunication. So we sat and visited for three hours while chaos went on outside of our little world.

She told me stories of coming to this part of the world to start a family and build a farm and I told her stories of my life as well. Her stories were better, and rich with old times and old ways, right down to the part where they had a fight over getting a tractor. She wanted to get a tractor to make his work a little easier. He wanted to use his horses because "they didn't pack the ground down as bad as those new fangled gizmos." She was living history, and I loved her stories and our time together.

But Shawn and her daughter did arrive, we did get the tire fixed, and we did have to say goodbye.

The second silver lining came in the form of something we had been looking for from the first flat… a heavy-duty tube! We had decided they didn't exist, but Shawn was grinning from ear to ear as he pulled the massive tube from its box. The box itself was four times larger than a regular tube box and the regular tubes felt paper thin compared to this "bad boy." We were both convinced our tube-popping days were over.

Shawn went one way to finish his tire fiasco, and I headed northeast as best as I could to the next river bordering the final state, New York. The Scenic Delaware starting at Hancock, New York, was my next water destination, but an hour and a half later in northern Scranton, the offset link broke again… my day was over.

I hadn't eaten all day, so I walked back a block to a local restaurant. It was really good, and I was really hungry. When Shawn arrived, I went and got the bike while Shawn ate. The owner of the restaurant said we could spend the night in the back parking lot away from the street, a relatively quiet place in the city to be. Not my choice, but very appreciated under the circumstances.

DAY 43—Vicki and Jesse Are Coming!

I was especially excited about today. If all went well, I should have an easy ride through beautiful hills and trees to Hancock, NY. There Vicki and my youngest son, Jesse, should meet me for the rest of the day and be with me for the last week of "Pedal-Paddle Across America" and the following week of "R&R" on Long Island.

My eyes automatically popped open at 7:00 a.m. in spite of a 1:00 a.m. bedtime the night before. I changed quickly and stepped outside to get started on the broken engine-side drive chain. In 30 minutes I had it taken care of and whirred down Business 6 North to Carbondale, where I was to take 171 North to 370 East.

It's a great ride high along the western river slope looking down into the valley and the city of Scranton. A quick stop for a fast-food breakfast and then gas took a lot longer than expected, both for the same great reason. Folks just have to know about Pedal-Paddle and the trip.

At one point a car of men passed around me yelling "hurrahs" for Columbia and then pulled over ahead of me and flagged me down. I spent a few minutes explaining and then passed out the last brochures I had on board.

Again I took off, and really, before I knew it I was crossing the bridge into New York! It was so sudden it literally took me by surprise. With all the problems of the day before, I'd just gone twice as far in three hours. It didn't seem possible.

The bridge was under repair and was open only as a single lane bridge with a traffic light to let one side go and then the other. It turned green on our side just as I got in line to go and I hardly slowed down to cross.

Once on the other side, I was in Hancock and pulled over in front of a hardware store to get a number 41 off-set link, in case it broke again, and to find out where I could get information about the Delaware River.

The hardware store directed me down the street another block to a fly-fishing and canoe trip specialty store. They were very friendly and helpful, and soon I had the knowledge I needed to make a good try at rafting the Delaware on a Pedal-Paddle.

The knowledge I got was a little scary, however; it seemed I could be in for the roughest ride of my trip. They were talking about No. 3 rapids with larger than three foot swells and irregular waves that could easily and suddenly swamp even a canoe expert…we'll see.

I also was informed that this little weekend getaway filled up quickly, so I got a recommendation for a little 17-room motel on the river and booked a room.

After checking in, I called around to find out Shawn was stuck in Scranton still but leaving soon, and Vicki and Jesse were just then getting up and around for the day. They were held up with storms and didn't get to bed till 4:30 a.m.

I killed time as best as I could for four hours. Shawn showed up about an hour before Vicki and Jesse.

It was really good to see them, and we found a local restaurant, as soon as possible. No one had eaten. After dinner we shot a few games of pool, something I seldom do, and then we decided between the only other two forms of entertainment in town, the bowling alley or the one movie. The movie won and afterward we ate again. These boys are 19 and 20 (Jesse turned 20 while we were going across Montana); what else are you gonna do but eat?

DAY 44—Happy Father's Day!

I got up and around, anxious to get on the Delaware River with my youngest son, Jesse. Vicki walked up and gave me a kiss and said, "Happy Father's Day." I didn't even know it was Father's Day! I was just glad they were there, and I had my son's company on the river, and all their company for dinner later, the formula for a great day.

We had a lot to do to get another Pedal-Paddle ready, but I didn't know Columbia had problems as well. When the back wheel was respoked, it was not put back on correctly, and almost all the paddles were broken before we caught the problem. I needed to get out by 8:00 a.m. to be off the river by dinnertime, so I couldn't believe it when we actually hit the water at 10:30 a.m.

My frustration vanished quickly once we were on the water. It was a beautiful clear river, so the fish, rocks, and plants were clearly in view as we skimmed over them. Sometimes four to five feet down, sometimes four or five inches, it was a great view for miles.

Jesse's enthusiasm for the trip and the scenery thrilled me. He seemed genuinely glad to be with me on the river for the day. He shouted and yelled at every fish sighting and really went nuts when we spotted our first bald eagle. Before the day was through, we spotted at least a dozen.

His only complaint was not having a fishing pole. He spotted fish after fish and tried to name each type. Pedal-Paddle's high seat vantage point is excellent for spotting things under the water, and Jesse remarked once he'd seen more fish in greater variety than in all his life. It was true. They seemed to be almost everywhere, and there were some whoppers, too. Before the day was up, we would see several fish over two feet long.

The weather was perfect with a north wind at 20 miles per hour or less, helping the river carry us south. The partly cloudy sky seemed to give us just the right variety of sun and shade throughout the day.

The river was perfect, too. It gave us choices to make around islands, fast water to excite us, and long still pools for us to paddle and just talk. It didn't take us long to tie the two units together. Now we were a twin-engine vehicle with Jesse on the right and me on the left. When we wanted to turn left he pedaled harder. When we wanted to turn right I pedaled harder. Steering became almost unnecessary as we cruised along together in near perfect harmony.

This whole scenario opened up the opportunity for conversations like we hadn't had in years, and we made the most of it, recalling past times and considering future plans. Jesse is a soul-mate to me. Vicki says he acts just like me. I doubt it's true, but we do share a special bond in a thousand areas just as my other son, Joab, and I have in a thousand other ways. They are so alike and yet so different and unique.

Strapped together for most of eight hours would be hell for some, but it was heaven for Jesse and me. It's not hard but impossible to describe what we saw, what we felt, and what we experienced on the river. All I can say is it was the absolute perfect Father's Day present from Jesse.

There's nothing I want more from my boys and my new daughter than some of their time, when they can.

We came off the river 20 miles shorter than I wanted for the day and nine miles shorter than our first planned connection for pickup. It was 6:00 p.m. and we would be on the river till dark to get the last nine miles. But there were Vicki and Shawn. They had been checking with the locals on our progress and had made a great decision to give us the opportunity to get off early. We took it and went and had a great dinner and conversation. After dinner, I went walking with Vicki on a dirt road that followed a creek up into the woods. It was Father's Day... Wow, what a great Father's Day!

Day 45 – No. 3 Rapids, Skinner's Falls!

I started the day with Shawn on the other Pedal-Paddle. It was a cool morning, so we pulled on a lot of clothes. The river was clothed as well, in a heavy fog on the water. It looked really mysterious and creepy, but strangely beautiful in its white swirling coat.

It was tricky as well, because we couldn't see the current or even the rocks until we were almost on top of them. The overcast sky added to the whole feel of the morning.

The first thing I did was to tie Shawn's Pedal-Paddle to Columbia. We became a stable twin-engine machine that was easy to keep straight in the water, just like Jesse and I were. The second thing we did was run up on a big rock. It was trickier than I thought! We got off the rock quickly, but not before my boots were both full of cold water that would remain for the next five hours.

We both marveled and put up with the unique conditions of the river for only a short while. Within an hour, we were pulling off our coats and laying them on the handlebars. What a quick change! The sun came out, the clouds all disappeared, and I mean *all*. The fog disappeared from the surface of the water as well. It was the most amazing thing. The sky went from totally overcast to totally blue.

Shawn spotted some deer and some bald eagles, and of course we saw fish of all kinds underneath our excellent little fish watching platforms.

The river was much faster than the day before, as well, with frequent #1 rapids. We hit one rapid that I felt should have been a #2. It was great! Big two-foot swells in a long run that threw me wildly about, but Columbia was so stable under me it was an easy task for it to remain stable the entire way down.

I went first to set up a camera shot for Shawn. He came down, got turned, and went through the violent water sideways, with what looked like as much stability and control as I had front ways. It was exciting to watch and thrilled me, as the inventor, to see my contraption in action.

All in all, it was a great ride with Shawn. He, like Jesse, was genuinely thrilled with the river, the ride, the nature and animals all around us; the whole experience.

In five hours we estimated we had gone about 25 miles, a good clip for human power combined with river flow. Just as we rounded the bend and saw the bridge, Vicki's rental car pulled along side us on the road. Jesse was hanging out the window screaming wildly with enthusiasm for seeing us on the water. He then yelled, "Left side after the bridge." We acknowledged and headed on down, but not until we emptied my left pontoon for the third time in the five hour trip.

We had to get off and walk the units a couple hundred feet in the shallows but pulled them up safely enough to leave them and walk up the hill for lunch.

Jesse gave the pontoon a good fix job while Shawn and I ate and Vicki had dessert. Then Vicki got ready to join me for the second stretch of water.

The second leg of the day's journey was to be only five miles, a perfect distance for Vicki's "all female" abilities. That may seem chauvinistic, but my wife is very feminine. She doesn't tent camp, hike much, or stuff like that, although she will try on occasion to be a "trooper" for my sake.

The problem is, it seems, that every time she tries, it blows up in my face and today was no different. These five miles turned out to be the slowest water I had seen in weeks. To top it off, a strange wind blew out of the south right into our faces on the half-mile long, still pools.

We struggled into the wind for a while, but it was no fun. Frankly, I became disgusted almost immediately. It reminded me of the nights she would agree to spend with me out on our sailboat. A sure formula for high winds or a thunderstorm!

Finally we pedaled for shore. I hooked a long rope to my seat while she tied the other end to her front tire. I fired up "the little engine that could," and I pulled her a good 40 feet behind me. Not at all the time, side by side in conversation and marveling at nature that I had with Shawn or Jesse. My forethought to bring rope was getting us down the river with her in tow. When I would look back she was smiling and looking around. I guess it was all right, just disappointing by comparison.

I pulled her along for about a mile and a half of the five to six miles of water, through two long still pools and a rapid. As we approached the next rapid, I switched off the engine and pulled her back up to me and tied her along side so we could go down together.

We had a nice little ride down that rapid, and we pushed into the wind through one more long pool.

Our bad ride wasn't quite over as we cut loose from each other to push our Pedal-Paddles over a large patch of thin water running over smooth round stones.

The ride finished on two good notes, however. The rocks ended out against a bank out of the wind and a beautiful stretch of water, and the bridge was where it was supposed to be! My, I wished she could have had a better ride! It was so unfair, it seemed, to be dealt that hand just when she didn't need it. Her ride was over, with very little nature and beauty as we concentrated on just being able to get down the river; something I'd spent a lot of time doing the last 43 days.

At the bridge, Vicki was off and Jesse was on in minutes. His pontoon fix was working great, so we didn't even dump the pontoons. Of course, the wind totally stopped and even came lightly to our backs once again. His enthusiasm always kicks my spirits up, and we went down the river, spotting fish, wildly excited to be on the river again.

The five miles to Skinner's Falls went quickly. So quickly, in fact we waited on Shawn and Vicki for about 30 minutes. The next five miles could take us right up to dark, so we decided we'd better go. Just as we were putting on our life jackets, we heard Shawn's voice. At least now they knew we'd been there and gone.

We shoved off; the #3 rapids were almost immediate. I knew I had more control with my little friend, so I flipped the switch on, pulled the cord and eased on down the river for a look. All I could see were boulders the size of our motor home with violent waterfalls crashing down between them.

I've learned something in life. I circled again. If I see water, I go. If I see boulders, I take out and go around. You'll always hit what you're looking at. I saw water!

I yelled at Jesse to hold back until I got all the way down, then I hit the first opening. I crashed down the waterfall easily, and my pontoons came right back up and stable. I hit the gas and circled the next pool, throwing the trademark 30-foot rooster tail as I went. I picked the next hole and dove into it with the same result. I went sideways, and the back grazed a boulder then straightened me up just as I went around it and over the third fall. I spun around to the right, feeling like it was over, and looked for Jesse. I spotted him at the top and then looked behind me quickly. One more boulder was right behind me, barely sticking up. I hit the throttle and pushed Columbia into the current. Of course, I was no match for its violent force, but it slowed my descent just enough to move left and around the boulder. I settled into the final flow of water in my backwards descent to watch what was sure to be the "Jesse show."

He hit the first fall perfectly, front down, and came right out of it. He pedaled violently, legs spinning to imitate my circle in the first pool. With less power, he made a three-quarter circle before the second fall grabbed him, and he went over it sideways! He must have balanced really well, because he just bobbed over it like it was nothing. His legs went to spinning as hard as he could, but the current was way too strong. He went over the third fall backwards! I saw him lean over the handlebars forwards with the same result as before. It looked effortless, the way the Pedal-Paddle went through near-death experiences and yet lived again!

When Jesse flowed down into the pool, we must have howled with laughter forever. Excited, we each battled to get in our version of what just happened to the two of us. All that was for sure was that both we and our Pedal-Paddles had survived.

Columbia had already gone through so much, I hated to do this to it, but it forgave me when it saw what a thrill I got out of the torture I put it through. It's like that, you know. So giving and forgiving.

Jesse and I tied alongside each other and continued to reminisce our recent near-death experience as we spotted more fish and even fresh water eels. We discussed the flow of the river from time to time and which way to go for the best and fastest ride. It was great fun.

Up ahead, we couldn't agree which way to go for the first time. Left looked good to Jesse but something about it bothered me. I studied it as we approached. There was a man in the middle of the stream. His pickup was on the left side, which meant he'd walked out there. Also, there was a big pole painted red on top in the small opening on the right side.

"Let's go right and hit that little opening," I said. Jesse responded to my "Dad decision" immediately.

The very second we went through the opening, it became clear what was going on and that we had made the right decision. I guess the local canoe and rafting companies got permission to do this. They had stacked rocks up in a big V across the river to make a little one to two foot dam. This raised that section of river up just enough to float, and the locals knew to hit that little opening on the right with a raft, canoe...or now a Pedal-Paddle. The man was in the middle clearing out what appeared to be a little narrow opening at the point of the V for a "canoe shoot." Just a guess or gut feeling on my part, but a good one. That's why I'm Daddy! Jesse complimented me on my decision, and that always feels good. We went on down the river as before, looking for fish, rocks, water plants or anything of special interest above water.

Jesse spotted a deer grazing in the approaching dusk of the day. He tried out his buck imitations and the doe turned to look at us. I teased him that she was in love as we floated on down, whisking away the newfound love of her life.

We had a great time, but it was over. We pulled out at Narrowsburg, a beautiful little village. After emptying out the pontoons and putting our units away for the night, Vicki drove us across the bridge to Pennsylvania where we ate like pigs, or at least us guys did. Five miles for Vicki, 25 for Shawn, and 10 for Jesse meant about 40 miles for me, almost all leg paddled. I was beat, but what a great day of memories!

DAY 46—Disconnected!

I left this morning with everybody in bed. Shawn had gotten up to help me get started but I knew where he was headed when I headed for the water. I guess they were all worn out. If you're not used to it, five, ten, and especially 25 miles is way too much to paddle, even down river.

It had rained off and on all early morning as I wrote "Day 45" while everyone slept, so I started out in a rain suit. Just a cheap top and bottom plastic thing in a bag, but it did the trick.

The clouds hung all over the hills as I pushed out into the river. It was still and peaceful, almost eerie as I started out. A light sprinkle on the water made it hard to read the current, and something some fresh water divers had told me added to the creepy feeling I had. They said the river, just beyond the bridge I was passing under, fell to 120 feet in depth, a huge hole for such a small river.

I got used to the whole mood change of the river after a while. Alone again, with my little friend pushing me along. The clouds that hung on the hills were really quite beautiful. Their movement was fascinating to watch as they crawled over the hills, sometimes left, sometimes right, sometimes climbing straight up and over. There must have been convection currents, but the apparent wind was driving their movement.

I went all morning without seeing a single fish, as the clouds kept the underwater world a dark mystery. Nothing but faint glimpses of the bottom were seen.

I grazed several rocks and a couple of boulders but nothing serious as I went along, often fooled by the ripples of the water and the rain. After about 20 miles in five hours, I came upon a bridge, a river coming in from Pennsylvania and a really nice paved ramp and parking lot on the Pennsylvania side. It was so accessible and clear, I thought surely this would be the place the crew would be ready to catch me, but no one was waiting for me there. I filled the tanks and checked the pontoons. The left one was shockingly full of water; I would guess over 50 pounds. Still, no one was there. I roamed up to the road on foot and saw I was at the Zane Grey Museum, and next to it was an old church and cemetery. I was wet, so I didn't want to go into the museum; besides, I couldn't see if they were to show up.

I wandered around the cemetery a bit. The grave of an unknown soldier of the revolutionary war was what caught my attention, buried in 1779, I think. Nothing in Amarillo is over 100 years old, and the sense of the history of this place started me thinking. All that America was to become started here. If this soldier could only see what his sacrifice had become. It really is amazing.

Still no one was here. What if they were just down below? I began to think of all the "what ifs" and decided to move on. I launched and headed down again. It was really a great ride. Lots of rapids, very little slow water; the kind of thrill ride the boys would love. Where were they?

If possible, it got prettier and faster, too. I passed several river accesses, both public and private, with canoe and raft rentals almost every mile, it seemed. I was the only craft I saw on the river all morning and now only one lone canoe in the afternoon.

High cliffs, wet with rain and green with moss, loomed overhead; a gorgeous sight. The rapids got bigger and the scenery more grand. Ahh, where were they? Jesse had one complaint of the #3 rapids the day before. "They were too short!" he had said. Here were great rapids a quarter mile, a half mile, even one three quarters of a mile long or so.

"Oh, I wish he were here," I agonized. I had seen such beauty all across the country with no one to share it with. This was killing me.
The bottom line is, they never found me. It was late evening and I was maybe an hour and a half from the end of the line for my Delaware River experience.

All of a sudden, the engine raced. I knew in an instant what that meant and hit the off switch to the engine. I looked back to see the chain rolling off the bottom sprocket into the river. I grabbed quick and caught it just as it was going off the end. Another offset link had broken. Lesson No. 1,734: never use offset links! But...I did get the chain.

I was worn plumb out, I had missed the rest of them all day and I had a piece of chain in my hand. I was pretty ticked. I forgot to mention I ended up emptying the pontoon every hour after the first 20 miles. Remember the V rocks the day before? I noticed one of those, so I ran the V to the tip to take the canoe shoot. It shot all right. At the end of it was a pile of rocks! I hit hard. With further inspection the side of the left pontoon was separated all the way through for a good 12 inches down the side. Wow, kind of amazing when you thick about it, but the way the pontoons are made with the top half almost the whole side wall, it traps air. One hour on a 12-inch separated side in a pontoon is nothing less than incredible. Anyway, it got me down the river.

In some way, the whole day was bittersweet. I hated being alone in such beauty and great water all day, but it *was* beautiful and great water.

At the end of the day, I just took Columbia out, pedaled or pushed it half a mile up the river access road and put it up. Rather than having my family sharing my day's experiences first hand, I was back to telling about them over dinner. By the way, their story was they spent all day looking for me. Doesn't seem possible, but that's the way the river can be. It's another world, one that until you've done it, you can only imagine. If you're like me, what you imagine is far from what it's really like.

DAY 47 – My Last Day of Land

I left Port Jervis after finding a regular # 41 chain link and making the necessary repair. I took off through Port Jervis on U.S. Highway 6, once again headed east for a point somewhere near Newburgh, N.Y., so I could get my last 50 miles on the Hudson River.

Everybody else wanted to see New York City for a couple of days, so I was going to try to get in 60 miles on land to Newburgh and then about 20 miles closer to the big city down the Hudson River. Then I could get the rest on the last day, Saturday, after just hanging out for a couple of days.

The ride was nice. Rolling hills, houses, and small towns. I rode a couple of hours, met up with Jesse and Shawn and pulled into a local Greek restaurant. Vicki and I had sailed the Greek Islands in a sailing flotilla as part of our 25th anniversary Europe tour. One thing led to another and the owner soon brought out pictures of islands we had been on and he had lived on. It thrilled him to meet someone that was familiar with what he called "my island." Vicki and I were equally thrilled to relive that part of our European vacation. The food was great and added to the memories. After a little more visiting and showing off Pedal-Paddle to several interested customers, it was time to go. I left first to get out ahead of them.

A New York state trooper stopped me to ask the same thing hundreds of people had asked. I explained what it was, who I was, and where I was going. He gave me his version of how I should get there, which I followed as best as I could. He either did not understand my inability for interstate travel or I simply didn't get the re-route correct, but in minutes I followed U.S. Highway 6 up onto an interstate-like U.S. 17 where they ran along together. Within a few more minutes, two more New York highway patrolmen were very graciously telling me I would have to take the next exit off, and just as nicely tried to re-route my re-route.

After a few tough hills in the Bear Mountain State Park area and some more beautiful scenery, I was at the U.S. Highway 6 bridge across the Hudson River. It looked to me to be a good half mile wide at this point with high hills on both sides. In fact, there seemed to be no way down to the river at all, except a little dock I spied down river, a part of the Bear Mountain State Park.

I went on a quest to get permission to get on the river. After the Chicago experience, I realized this is not the west and there are rules for everything. In this case I was told to "do it, just don't tell us about it," an answer that was good enough for me and, I thought, real nice of the park official on duty.

I followed their instructions to the docks, the last part of which was a walking path that went down a steep hill and under the riverside railroad tracks. It was five feet wide and wheel chair accessible, just barely passable for Pedal-Paddle, but we got down fine. The best way to the water was over a four-foot wall to sometimes large rolling wakes. A ship and a barge had just passed by.

A man fishing with his son, who displayed a classic New York attitude, reluctantly dropped his fishing pole to help me lift Columbia over the wall and into the water so Vicki wouldn't have to. She handed me my two gas cans, and I got immediately away from the wall. I tied the tanks onto the front left pontoon brace as I moved out into the river, looked back to wave at Vicki and moved on down the river.

After seeing two such large vessels on the river, I was a little nervous, but pleasure boats and a couple of playful jet skis settled me down a bit. I concluded it might be less than death defying to be out there with the "big boys."

For the first few miles, I floated past the beautiful shores of the park. After that, I mostly passed by factories: one big riverside plant of some sort after another. One such plant had a ship along side seemingly unloading coal for electrical generation. The river, already wider than the biggest lake in the area I'm from, opened three times wider to maybe three or four miles wide. It was really spectacular as I rounded the bend to see what looked like a hundred sailboats on the water. There were boats of all kinds, and more jet skis, too, but the sails with the evening sun at my back showed with such definition in the distance it was quite a sight.

I went on for a while further but hailed an inquisitive jet-ski rider to direct me to the nearest down river marina. He gave directions and even called my wife with directions on where to meet me on shore. After I told my story, he and his two quiet little riding buddies sped off, and before I knew it, I was swarmed with jet skis and cameras. It was quite flattering to get such a reaction from jet ski enthusiasts.

I made my way to the marina, then to the dock. A nice gentleman at the dock asked my story and insisted on helping me and getting me tide charts for the rest of my trip down the Hudson. The Hudson is a tidal flow river this close to the New York Harbor, and flow depends strictly on the tides. Low tide to high tide flows "up stream," high tide to low tide flows down, with a little variation depending on how far upriver you are. I thanked him for his help and went my way looking for a place to keep Columbia for the night.

It was too far to the motel we were to end up at that evening, ten miles inland, but a marina service vender offered me a piece of shop floor space to bed Columbia down for the night. I took it and headed for food and sleep.

DAY 48—A Day Off?

So much for a day off! I hadn't had but one real day off since we started, unless you count the one with Vicki scouting out Mississippi River locks and dams; all part of the job, really.

I promised to be at the man's shop between eight and nine a.m. to get Columbia. Jesse and I took the big motorcycle and made a "father and son" morning out of it. He's still young and crazy – I drove. We had a great, pleasurable, but cool ride through the hills and neighborhoods of the New York City suburbs.

Even though I'm a "big cities are to visit only" kind of guy, I was really impressed with what living 20 miles out of the city might be like. It was quite pleasant and...natural. We made our way to the marina, grabbed Columbia with a hearty "thank you" and headed out. A fast-food breakfast was calling us, so we found a local McDonald's and ate. Then we split up for the trek back to the motel.

Our motel was on U.S. Highway 59, more like a six lane city street than anything. I stayed safely to the right as I had done for 3,000 miles. Traffic was building up on the right for a major highway exit and our motel was on the left.

With no one in the left lanes, I used my bright orange gloves to point left twice, pulled up on the median, waited for traffic in the other direction to pass and moved off the median into our motel.

I was visited there by one, then two, then three suburb city police cars. Normally a friend, advocate, and supporter of the police, I was frankly treated with a total lack of understanding and respect, followed by 30 minutes of trying their absolute best to go through the home office rulebook by radio. Finding nothing, they came back with a few false accusations, threats and general bull, handed me back my license and let me go. I apologized "for anything I may have done or said" that might have caused three police cars to give me 30 minutes of their precious time. How many police does it take to look at a bicycle with pontoons anyway? To be clear, all I did was apologize at the time. The rest are my comments of the situation to you, the reader. I would suggest you always do the same. Police do have a tough job. Even if they don't handle it very well from time to time, they're still in authority and deserve and need our respect. This whole incident was clearly a case of abuse of authority and nothing else...thus, the unnamed town...finally, finding nothing wrong, they let me go.

For the rest of the day, I got cleaned up and headed for New York for a media conference and planning session. With such tight schedules, it was decided that I would follow the river to the 79th Street boat basin tomorrow, Friday, and the short run on land from the boat basin to Times Square on Saturday. This would leave time Saturday morning for interviews, demonstrations and photo opportunities on the water immediately followed by more of the same on land. So much for a day off!

I was apprehensive but anxious for my last piece of water. The Hudson down to the boat basin on Manhattan Island has its own brand of treachery. Tomorrow I trade rapids and rocks for currents, ships, barges, big water and possible wind, waves, and wake swells the size of houses. The range and variety of dangers on this trip have been astronomical! See you tomorrow....

DAY 49—New York, New York, Big City, Big Surprises!

This day, my last, would be full of big surprises, some bad, some good. The first big surprise was how late we got out… not good. I had allowed a late night in New York with views from the Empire State Building at night, etc. I was repaid with a crew that wasn't ready and couldn't get motivated while my friendly current was slipping away; not at all good. After much preparation, some that was supposed to have been done the night before (namely recaulking the pontoons) I hopped on Columbia in a mad panic to beat the current, while Jesse went ahead on the motorcycle to scout a place to get in a little farther down river. Vicki followed so we could get an immediate response to anything that might fail on the way to the water.

Just as I was pulling into a riverside state park, one of many, a vehicle with a kayak on top pulled in behind me. I proceeded to stop one of the nicest and most helpful New Yorkers you'll ever find. He led us at my speed through winding streets, right down to a private little water access. It was perfect, and then he gave me every bit and piece of information I would need for a successful trip, while Jesse, Vicki, and I prepared Columbia for launch.

I yelled a "thank you" back for the gazillionth time, as I pushed off the shore. My friendly Hudson River guide, Vicki and Jesse went for coffee. Is life fair? Actually they're the ones who got cheated.

The next big surprise of the day was the natural beauty. On the New Jersey shore were high cliffs and steep, wooded hills. Nothing but natural beauty, very untamed and unspoiled, except for a couple of marinas and a little public beach.

The New York side was more like I would have expected. It had lower hills, apartments, high-rise buildings of all sorts, and industry. Increasing all the time on the left side of me were the buildings and factories while the natural beauty of the New Jersey shore continued all the way to the George Washington Bridge.

Wow! What a bridge! Even in the limited visibility of the New York City air I could see the bridge ten miles away. It was huge from the water and just got bigger and bigger.

As I chugged towards it, several large yachts cruised by in both directions, one barge and one ship. The next big surprise was the ship and barge wakes. They were so wide between swells that I just rolled up and down like an elevator. The big yachts were just the opposite. Their wakes were big and choppy and sent me for a wild ride every time.

The weather was pleasant for the most part with occasional breezes, but just like in the small rivers, when the wind blew against the current it caused swells. What I had at one point was three foot swells with two-foot waves on top of the swells. Not really all that bad until a swell and a wave happened together. Then it got a little crazy. At least it was just every once in a while instead of the constant pounding I got on Lake Michigan.

I reached the last little beach on the Jersey shore a mile and a half before the bridge, just as my guide said I would. I pulled out to fill the tanks and empty the pontoons, but not before answering a few genuinely friendly questions for the harbor patrol. They seemed to enjoy my story immensely and gave me no words but that of encouragement.

I answered several more questions for excited and curious folks on the Jersey shore as I readied Columbia for what was supposed to be her final little six mile walk in the park to the 79th Street boat basin.

Checking in with Vicki by phone briefly, I pushed back off and immediately started heading across the mile-wide river to the far shore pillars of the George Washington Bridge. It was spooky not being able to see clearly up or down the huge river. The ships and barges were so fast compared to me; it would take constant appraisal of the horizon just to keep out of danger. It seemed like it took forever to cross, but the bridge supports got closer and closer and no ships appeared until I had made it all the way across and was safely against the Manhattan Island shore.

My first impression of how large the bridge was at a distance was elevated to new heights as I passed under it just off the Manhattan Island shore. The roar of the traffic above me, even though it loomed so high overhead, drowned out the engine noise right behind my seat. It was like a giant roadway was stretched between two unfinished skyscraper frames.

Just past it, the shore swept back into a shallow cove and back out again, not as a natural cove, but because a huge concrete structure protruded several hundred feet out into the water. The closest distance between two points is a straight line, so I headed straight for the outer corner of the building.

The next big surprise was the worst of all. I was half way between the bridge and the building that protruded so far out in the water when I had a strong sense that I wasn't moving.

I checked my forward progress by lining up near and far trees on the bank and sure enough I was right! The hour I got started late was about to cost me dearly. The tide had turned and it was like throwing everything in reverse. I expected there to be a time of stagnation between tide flows, but it was almost immediate. One minute the "bay-like river" flowed towards the ocean, the next minute it flowed up stream. Just like that!

I angled towards shore to get in behind the building. It blocked the flow a little, but I was literally crawling up the bank with four miles to go. I had a little throttle left so I gave it all it had and began to angle back out around the building. As I came to the corner and into the full current you could measure my progress in inches per minute. It was a snail's pace.

Just when I thought it couldn't get any worse, the engine quit. I reached back to pull at the cord a couple of times, but the current grabbed me so quickly I was headed the wrong way fast. I struggled to get control and pedaled hard for the wall. I found some steel bars and tied Columbia to the wall with some rope I had in my bag. It banged the wall with every wake swell, but I had to have time to think.

I adjusted the throttle, primed the engine and pulled the cord again. It fired!

I quickly untied the rope and hit the throttle. I began to move forward inches at a time again for a few feet, and it quit again. Again I tied it up, messed with it and again it fired, only to quit again after a few feet.

In a mixture of frustration and desperation, I began pulling Columbia hand-over-hand, along the wall, trying hard to keep it from banging in the process.

After 100 feet or so, I tried the engine again. It fired and pulled ahead slowly as before.

Somehow, and I'm not sure how, I noticed the back tire was splashing up on the engine so I tied off the throttle, steered with the left hand, and reached back with my right hand to cover the air intake partially and block the water spray.

I inched forward in this way for a long time as the wind now started to get up and make waves as well. There were times when the wind added to the current and I would go nowhere, then it subsided just enough to allow me a little gain. All in all, it was miserable, and where before I was ready to make a 1:30 p.m. landfall, I was now wondering if I would make the last couple of miles at all.

I called on my cell to give my location to Patrick and Vicki and see if we could find a way and a place to pull Columbia out on the big rocks and boulders that now lined the shore. It seemed like forever as we ground out a few feet at a time with press and TV news alerted to what was supposed to be a 2:00 p.m. arrival at the 79th Street boat basin on Manhattan Island. I was in fear for Columbia as well. It had been hours now since I had stopped to check the pontoons for water, and the caulk that had been applied early this morning was beginning to wash off. The waves and boat wakes continued to wash over the pontoons like a boxer exploiting his opponent's wounded eye.

The whole situation was relentless, devastating, frustrating, demoralizing, fear-creating, and totally avoidable, by simply getting out on time this morning, a thought that compounded my agony with both regret and fault finding.

Crawling along the edge of the park now, I stayed just off the rocks, apologizing to every face behind every fishing pole as I unavoidably disrupted their favorite spot. I tried hard to smile and look in control, even though I felt out of control, both in emotion and in my circumstance.

I looked up after a long while, and there was Patrick, Shawn, and Jesse on shore waving. Patrick was videotaping while Jesse shouted encouragement. Although half of me was sure I was going down for the last time, the other half suddenly felt like I was going to mysteriously somehow make it. The pontoons felt heavy in the water. I was making almost no head way at all. The waves continued to bob me up and down and break over the half-sunk pontoons.

I couldn't hear what they were shouting at me, but their facial expressions and gestures indicated I was actually making it. I crawled down the rocky shoreline another mile in this same half-whipped fashion to an anchored barge that served as a platform for something. As I slowly swung out to go around it, I could tell the current strengthened its resolve to keep me from my goal, but "the little engine that could" kept screaming "I think I can, I think I can, I think I can." I could see only inches at a time go by as we struggled to clear the end of the barge. Then one mile ahead, I recognized the cluster of boats that signaled the position of the 79th Street boat basin and our landing dock, the end of the trip for Columbia and me.

As I came around the end of the barge, I angled closer and closer to shore. The current began to lose more and more, and I could almost hear the chant turn to "I know I can, I know I can, I know I can!" Its speed slowly increased to a walking pace and the three disappeared, no doubt to meet my now sure arrival.

I sat up more and more, as it became increasingly less necessary to streamline myself in the wind. The boats and docks of the boat basin protected me more and more from both the current and the wind. I was cruising at a good brisk walk now, sitting up high and waving back at all the New York City Park spectators. It was more than just a good feeling. It was finishing strong, with pride and dignity. A fight well fought, and a race well run.

We had not cheated. We had gone every mile, fully amphibious. Ready at all times on water to go to land, and ready at all times on land to go to water. No regrets, no compromises, fully accomplishing what we set out to prove. A basic under-$1,000 toy with the added engine option had just crossed America on both land and water.

On water we had skimmed over rocks in four inches of water, shot #3 rapids, weathered three-foot white caps and 30 miles per hour wind gusts. On land we had fought side winds, head winds, hills, bad pavement, traffic, two mountain passes, and all that can be thrown at a little, fragile vehicle. It had been given the rubble-striped, debris-strewn, potholed side of the road and yet survived.

As we pulled Columbia out of the water, pontoons at least 50 pounds overweight with water each, I vowed never to ask it to go back again. I was so proud of my invention. It did what I asked it to do and then some. It had taken it all on, for 4,000 miles, like no vehicle had ever done before, and came through the other side, victoriously!

Tomorrow is nothing more than a three-mile parade to Time Square, and this is all Columbia will ever do again, *parades*! It is my sincere wish that Columbia and I be used from this day forward in parades and in whatever way might present itself, to remind kids always to wear bright colored clothing and a bright colored helmet when riding. A reminder of safety to get them down the road as I have just done from sea to shining sea all across this incredibly diverse and beautiful country of ours, *safely*!

God bless,
Jay Perdue

A Summary of Pedal-Paddle's Performance

I know I'm the inventor, and as such, much of what I have to say may be taken lightly, so let the facts speak for themselves. This unit went 4,000 miles without any problems at all except the following.

First flat at 500 miles
$20 cassette at 2,500 miles
Re-gluing the pontoons in places at 3,000 miles
Little one inch breaks at the end of the top structure bumps put into the plastic from 3,000 miles to the end.

We continued to have flats. The roadside debris and overall condition of the road shoulders was appalling, except on the interstates where we were not allowed from Minnesota on. Shawn found heavy-duty tubes and the problem stopped.

"The little engine that could" really did most of the work, meaning the cassette had to "free-wheel" most of the time, something a standard bike simply is not required to do. It was a small price to pay for all the work the engine did.

Three thousand miles is not bad, but I know Pedal-Paddle, Inc., will do a better job as we gain experience in gluing the two halves of the pontoons together. The good news is, since the top overlaps the bottom, they continued to float for over an hour at a time even though at one time I banged several boulders in the rapids of the Delaware River and had a one-foot separation!

The "strength bumps" that go across the top of the pontoons need to go to the very edge, and the mold is being changed to see that they do.

That's it! An under-$1,000 toy with a $600 engine took on 4,000 miles of rough roads, potholes and all types of water conditions and won! Really won! No doubt the pontoon attachment points had to have been wallowed out from all the vibration and banging around, but it held together, performed well all the way, and didn't flip or dunk me once. Nor did I wreck once. I arrived in New York without a single scratch on me in spite of probably a hundred death-defying experiences.

All in all, inventor or not, Pedal-Paddle amazed me. Its durability, stability, and versatility are unequaled in the water toy world. A solid value, in many ways worth much more than the "asking price."

Jay Perdue

About the Author

Jay Perdue is or has been an inventor, song writer, lecturer, drummer, children's church leader, song leader, designer and builder of earth shelter structures and wind generators, recording engineer and producer, and all-around crazy guy who will do almost any (legal and moral) thing, backed up by his equally talented and beautiful wife, Vicki, of 28 years. Jay owns 6 patents, mostly in the field of acoustics. Their corporation, Jayvic, Inc., owns Perdue Acoustics and supplies the best and best-valued acoustical products on the market to schools, churches and other facilities worldwide.

The Perdues, along with their son, Joab, and new daughter-in-law, Melissa, also own Pedal-Paddle, Inc. It all started when Jay and his sons, Joab and Jesse, built their first primitive amphibious bikes for themselves. Now the company can furnish the public with 13 different models of amphibious bikes. One of the models is just like Pedal-Paddle Columbia! It's a rare thing to be able to buy a copy of a machine that set so many records and for so little money!

Jayvic, Inc., also owns Jayvic Publishers which handles all of Jay's children's songs and books of various topics, including a science fiction novel, *The Chainge*, a must-read thriller. One belief Jay holds strongly is that God is the giver of "inspired ideas and witty inventions," according to the book of Proverbs, and he has written a book entitled *Proverbs 8:12: I, wisdom, dwell with prudence, and find out knowledge of witty inventions*, a very insightful book into the how's, where's, and when's of inventive and creative thought. Jay loves to lecture on this subject as well.

Jay, Vicki, Joab and Melissa also own their own Perdue Recording Studios, a facility utilized primarily for their personal projects. "Will the GoWilla" is Jay's favorite project soon to come out on cassette, CD and even video with his very own programmed mechanical gorilla, so life-like, it will make you wonder!

For any interest in any of these and "more to come" projects, log onto perdueacoustics.com, pedal-paddle.com or jayvicpublishers.com or call or write the numbers listed below.

Thank you and God bless!

Perdue Acoustics
4210 Hester Drive
Amarillo, TX 79124
(806) 374-9402

Pedal-Paddle, Inc.
4212 Hester Drive
Amarillo, TX 79124
(806) 373-9402